HOW TO GET EXECUTIVES TO ACT FOR
PROJECT SUCCESS

BUILDING A STRONG MUTUAL PARTNERSHIP

MICHAEL O'BROCHTA

How To Get Executives To Act For Project Success

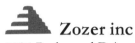 Zozer inc

3226 Peakwood Drive
Roanoke, VA 24014
(540)343-1883
www.zozerinc.com

PMI®, PMP®, PMI-ACP®, and *The PMBOK® Guide* are registered marks of the Project Management Institute, Inc.

ISBN: 978-1981283439

DEDICATION

This book is dedicated to my wife, who is the most well-read person I know. And, it is dedicated to our son, who is the hardest-working and smartest person I know. What a terrific combination.

.

CONTENTS

ABOUT THE AUTHOR

Michael O'Brochta, PMI-ACP, PMP, has managed hundreds of projects and hundreds of project managers during the past thirty-plus years. He is an experienced leader, manager, author, presenter, trainer, and consultant. He holds a master's degree in engineering management and a bachelor's degree in electrical engineering. As Zozer inc founder and president, his consulting expertise is helping organizations raise their level of project management performance. As senior project manager at the Central Intelligence Agency, he led the development of highly complex, top-secret projects, programs,  and systems; he also led the development of their project management and systems engineering training and certification program to mature practices agency-wide. Additionally, he led the development of standards and courses for the new U.S. Federal Acquisition Certification for Program and Project Managers.

Mike recently served at the PMI corporate level as Chair of the Ethics Member Advisory Group where he directed the tenfold expansion in outreach and the development of the ethical decision-making framework; he is a graduate of the PMI Leadership Institute Master Class. He has written and presented papers each of the past 17 years at PMI Global Congress events as well as at hundreds of international and regional conferences. Topics that he is currently passionate about include great project managers, quiet leadership, and why bad projects are so hard to kill. Since his recent climb of another of the world's seven summits, he has been exploring the relationship between project management and mountain climbing. Mike has been featured in PMI Today, PM Network, ProjectManagement.com, CIO Magazine, Information Week, and Government Executive Magazine, published hundreds of articles and papers, and co-authored a half-dozen project management books.

Chapter 1

INTRODUCTION

"A lot of good arguments are spoiled by some fool who knows what he is talking about."
Miguel de Unamuno 1864-1936
Spanish essayist

Even world-class project managers will not succeed unless they get their executives to act for project success. The trap of applying best-practice project management only to have the project fail because of executive inaction or counteraction can be avoided. According to the latest *PMI Pulse of the Profession*[1] report, "actively engaged executives continue to be the top driver of whether projects met their original goals and business intent." Increasing numbers of project managers are trying to deal with this reality.

This is a how-to book. It describes how project managers can get their executives to act, and it identifies executive actions most likely to contribute to project success. This book explores why the evolving and expanding definition of project success and why the expanding complexity of projects have led to an environment in which the project manager is ever more dependent on the executive. It draws upon recent research about top performing project managers, about why executives fail, and about why new products fail, to identify the basis for a strong mutual partnership between project managers and executives. A central theme is that project managers are empowered to extend their influence beyond the immediate project boundaries up into the organization, not only to get their executives to act, but also to help implement the actions as well.

The impact of organizational maturity, organizational change readiness, and the differing viewpoints and communication styles between executives and project managers are related to the timing and pace for the executive actions. Information is drawn from research in related fields of management, leadership, and organizational behavior. A model is offered to help the project manager gauge levels of executive support for projects, and a list of steps are identified that the project manager can take to accelerate executive support to the next level. A project management council and a project champion role are described as key approaches for project managers to use to amplify their influence to get executives to act.

This book's organization and flow is linear as depicted in Figure 1.1. First, we look at problems that contribute to the need for executive action, and then, we look at the actions executives can take for project success. With those understandings, we examine the barriers and limitations that executives may encounter as they contemplate taking some of those actions. Finally, we examine what steps project managers can take to help executives overcome the barriers so that the executives can actually take some of the actions that will contribute to project success. A strong mutual partnership underpins the relationship between the project manager and the executive.

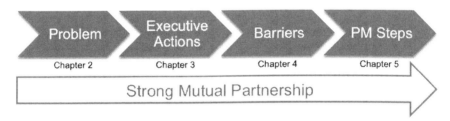

Figure 1.1 – Book Organization

I have written this book for the same reason I have written so many papers, articles, and publications: I am stimulated by project success. That stimulation involves finding ways to help other project managers achieve more success more of the time. And by success, I am referring to the success not only of their own projects and careers, but also to the success of others and to the success of the organization in which they work.

I became stimulated by this subject about 30 years ago when, as an engineer and project management employee of the Central Intelligence Agency, I enjoyed the rare privilege of a full year off with pay to undertake an advanced degree of my choice at the university of my choice, all expenses paid. It was during my studies at George Washington University toward a Master in Engineering Management degree[2] that my eyes were opened in a significant way; it was as if I had received a pair of special CIA x-ray glasses and could see things clearly that previously were fuzzy or invisible. While earning that degree, I studied *Management of Organizational Behavior* by Paul Hersey and Kenneth Blanchard.[3] That book provided me with an appreciation for the importance of the behavioral sciences. Thereafter, in addition to my perspectives as an engineer and as a project manager, I adopted the perspective of a organizational behaviorist. At the end of the day, I feel that project management is as much, or more, about people and relationship management as it is about the management of tasks.

About 15 years ago, when I began seriously looking into the available literature on the subject of executive actions for project success, I realized that it had received limited attention. At that time, to oversimplify a bit, much more attention was being paid to project management fundamentals, such as those found in the second edition of the *Guide to the Project Management Body of Knowledge* from the Project Management Institute.[4] At that time, project management was busy trying to identify and communicate its business value. Fortunately, a couple of forward-leaning authors had begun to explore the intersection of project management with executives.[5] Of particular note is a book published in 1997 by Robert Graham and Randall Englund titled *Creating an Environment for Successful Projects*[6] and a paper published in 2000 by Gary Heerkens titled *How to Implement Project Management in Any Organization.*[7] We can thank these gentlemen for shining an early light on this important subject. More recently, we can thank co-authors Timothy Kloppenborg, Debbie Tesch, and Chris Manolis for conducting research about this subject. Their 2014 paper titled *Project Success and Executive Sponsor Behaviors: Empirical Life Cycle Stage Investigations* advanced our understanding of this subject as it relates to project phases.[8] Most recently, we can thank PMI for including, for the first time, a section in *The PMBOK® Guide* that addresses the environment in which projects operate.[9] My understanding of this topic has benefited from a significant number of direct interactions with project managers and with executives. Much of that interaction has been associated with the myriad papers and presentations I have given; indeed, this is the most popular topic about which I have written or spoken. The topic of executive actions for project success has also been central in much of my consulting business. I have incorporated relevant aspects from these publications and others, as well as from the interactions, in this book; chapter end notes are included for readers interested in further exploration.

Stories are integrated into the book where I feel they contribute to the understanding of an important point. The stories, unless otherwise indicated, are fictional composites. They do describe actual people and actual events, and they do accurately represent the facts, but for the sake of clarity and brevity, they have been edited and combined in a way that does not strictly adhere to reality.

Exercises with sample solutions are provided to help you advance to higher levels of learning and to assist you in applying the information in this book within your organization. These exercises can be performed individually or together with other members of your organization.

I have also included an appendix written for executives. It presents the essential elements of this book in a form and tone that has been tailored to their needs. Since this appendix is a stand-alone body of work, you could give it to an executive to read to help advance the building of a strong mutual partnership focused on executive actions for project success.

I would be honored to receive comments, questions, or information from interested readers and to have the opportunity to include that information, with attribution, in a future publication.

Chapter End Notes

[1] Project Management Institute. (2017). *Pulse of the profession: success rates rise*. Newtown Square, PA: Project Management Institute. This global survey publication, which is part of a series that began in 2006, reported that the relationship between executives and project managers must be founded on transparency and trust and must recognize that there is a high degree of interdependence.

[2] George Washington University was one of the first institutions in the country to offer an advanced degree in what now is generally referred to as project management. The chairman of the department responsible for that degree program was J. Davidson Frame; he currently serves as the Academic Dean of the University of Management and Technology and as a member of the Project Management Institute Board of Directors.

[3] Hersey, P., & Blanchard, K. (1988). *Management of organizational behavior (fifth edition)*. Englewood Cliffs, NJ: Prentice-Hall. This book is now in its tenth edition.

[4] PMI membership in the year 2000 when the second edition of the PMBOK® Guide was released was about 30,000; today, the organization has released six editions of that document and has almost 500,000 members.

[5] I have had the distinct pleasure of spending time with and getting to know each of these noteworthy authors. Their thought leadership continues to inspire many and move the project management profession forward.

[6] Graham, R., & Englund, R. (1997). *Creating an environment for successful projects*. San Francisco, CA: Jossey-Bass. A second edition of this book was published. Randall Englund, together with co-author Alfonso Bucero, published a follow-on book in 2012 titled *The Complete Project Manager: Integrating People, Organizational, and Technical Skills*.

[7] Heerkens, G. (2000*). How to implement project management in any organization*. PMI Annual Seminars & Symposium 2000. Houston, TX. This paper included a list of five essential ingredients to establish a project management culture.

[8] Kloppenborg, T., Tesch, D., & Manolis, C. (2014, February/March). Project success and executive sponsor behaviors: empirical life cycle stage investigations. *Project Management Journal*. Newtown Square, PA: Project Management Institute. The research findings suggested that during the executing stage, project sponsors should focus on ensuring communications as a top priority.

[9] Project Management Institute. (2017). *A guide to the project management body of knowledge (PMBOK®) (sixth edition)*. Newtown Square, PA: Project Management Institute. This edition includes a new 9-page section focused on the environment in which projects operate that lists internal and external factors that can impact the project. The publication also includes treatment of stakeholder management, a topic that has been updated since it first appeared in the previous edition.

.

Chapter 2

EXAMINE THE PROBLEM

"A problem well stated is a problem half solved."
Charles Kettering 1876-1958
American inventor

The Problem

On many occasions, I have opened my presentations on the subject of getting executives to act for project success as follows:

> "For the moment, I am going to assume that each and every member of the audience is a world-class project manager who understands and uses all of the best practices in *The PMBOK® Guide* and elsewhere. There are no project managers anywhere who are more skilled and experienced than you. Congratulations, you are the best of the best. I'm honored to be able to speak to you. There is just one problem: you can not succeed. Your projects are doomed to fail. Why? Because you can not do it alone, you are dependent on your executive. You can not succeed unless you get your executive to act for project success."

Since the opening can seem a bit dramatic, it grabs the attention of the audience, and it succinctly makes the point about the importance of executive actions for project success. Project managers who continue doing what used to work by focusing within the bounds of the project are now finding success more difficult to achieve. The problem is that project success is dependent, to an increasing degree, not only on the efforts of the project manager, but on the efforts of the executive as well. This explains why three-quarters of the employees surveyed by the Towers Perrin[1] organization in a large global study said, "that their organizations or senior management don't do enough to help them fully engage and contribute to their companies' success." And it explains why, when U.S. federal government project managers were asked about executive support for a study conducted by the Council of Excellence in Government, 80% responded that they were not getting what they needed.[2] Plus, when PricewaterhouseCoopers conducted their 2012 global survey on the state of project management,[3] they found that "lack of executive sponsorship was the second largest factor that contributed to poor project performance." Jack Welch, former CEO of General Electric, is reported to have gone so far as to have said, "If you can't get top management to support your program, don't even try."

Anecdotally, these compelling statistics are evidenced through the collective experiences of the thousands of project managers whose reaction to useful information from a class or conference includes some form of "I wish my boss could have learned this." They are lamenting the gap that exists between what they need to succeed as project managers and what they are getting from their executives. The problem for these project managers is understanding how to get executives to act for project success.

This problem is illustrated in Figure 2.1 with a story about "George," or "Georgette" if you prefer. Surveys and research suggest that there are many stories such as this. The story is about a project manager who thinks he knows what needs to be done but does not think that he can do it. The story is about a project manager who is trying what may have worked in the past only to find it does not work now. The story is about a project manager who feels he lacks authority or power to overcome the "system." And, the story is about a project manager who looks at his executive as a contributor to the problem instead of someone

George, a project manager who is trying to apply some recently acquired knowledge, related how frustrated he was after learning about the best practice technique of writing a project charter. He was enthusiastic about how such a document could help him establish and maintain his authority, an aspect of his job with which he was consistently having trouble. However, he lamented that he could never use such a document because the part of the organization he worked in had not, and would not, adopt such a technique.

Figure 2.1 – Problem Story

with whom he can build a strong mutual partnership to take actions for project success.

In my many years as a project manager, as a manager of project managers, and as a project management consultant, I have heard countless stories like this one. Often, the project manager who has experienced this type of frustration has adopted the mantle of a victim. In that regard, he or she has learned through negative reinforcement that there is little to be done about the situation other than to accept it as is. For him or her, the glass is half empty. Perhaps so. For me and I hope for the majority of the readers of this book, the glass is half full. I take responsibility for making the best of whatever situation I find myself in, not only for myself, but also for my co-workers and for the organization in which I am working. I genuinely believe that it is my responsibility to take some initiative to help reduce the likelihood that the next "George or Georgette" will experience the lack of executive support necessary for project success.[4]

The Context

The topic of getting executives to act falls within the broader context of the topic of project success; after all, project success is our primary reason for seeking executive action. If we visualize this context as a progression, then early in the process we can focus on examining the first-order criteria for project success, and we can then examine the actions we can take as project managers to cause the project to be successful. This view of the progression represents the traditional bounds of project management and is fairly well represented in *The PMBOK® Guide* and other readily available authoritative sources. History has shown this to be a relatively effective approach to project management for the types of projects with relatively low complexity, limited dependencies, and well-defined scope.

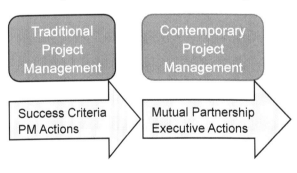

Figure 2.2 – Contemporary PM

However, an increasing number of projects and programs do not fit this rather narrow view. Project complexity is rapidly increasing and so are the number of project dependencies. Scope definitions are expanding, and they can be increasingly vague, at least at the outset. This expanding definition of success now includes second-order factors well beyond the immediate control or influence of the project manager. In addition to the traditional project manager actions, executive actions must also be taken to support the efforts of the project manager as illustrated in Figure 2.2. This consideration now takes the topic of project success to an entirely new level. This new level involves focusing outside the traditional bounds of the project to form a mutual partnership with executives. It involves focusing on the executive; it involves focusing on getting the executive to act for project success.

It is important to note that in the results-oriented culture that encompasses so many organizations undertaking projects, the success of the project manager is largely dependent on the success of the project. A project that successfully delivers its product or service will likely also deliver a career boost for the project manager. Conversely, a failed project, regardless of how well it might have been managed, can stall or derail a project manager's career. Like it or not, project managers are known by the outcome of their projects.[5]

Executive Definition

For the purpose of conveying the concepts in this book, I have adopted a broad definition for the executive as shown in Figure 2.3. I am defining an executive as somebody responsible for the administration of a business or department. This executive may be an individual or a function performed by more than

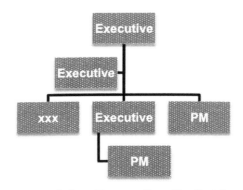

Figure 2.3 – Executive Definition

one individual, such as a board or committee. It could even be a project management office. On an organization chart, the executive appears above other individuals and functions, including the project manager. The executive could be a project manager's boss, a sponsor, a senior stakeholder, a business or department head, or a vice president. Ultimately, the executive is someone with more authority and power than the project manager. An executive who is focused on the business operations and processes associated with the department in which the project resides would be a likely candidate to act for project success. Ideally, this executive is positioned close enough to the project work to be able to have a genuine impact. Ideally, this executive believes as I do, that his or her job is to create a culture for project success.[6]

Success Definition Expanded

Project success is tough to achieve. The often-cited *Chaos Report* from the Standish Group shows that 71% of information technology projects are still outright failures or challenged to the point of not meeting the time/cost/quality triple constraint.[7] The statistics are equally dim for non-IT types of projects. For many project managers, the situation is even worse because the definition of project success has expanded beyond the triple constraint used for the Chaos data to the point of being far harder to achieve.

In the 1960's, the early days of modern project management, success was likely to be measured entirely in technical terms. Either the deliverable product worked or it did not. During the 1970's, that narrow definition was expanded to encompass completion on time, within cost, and at an acceptable level of quality. This has become known as the triple constraint and has been widely used as the basis for much of the project management industry. During the 1980's, further expansion took place to include criteria relating to customer acceptance. And during the 1990's, still more criteria were added, having to do with the main work flow of the organization, the corporate culture, and the strategic business objectives.[8] Figure 2.4 depicts this historical progression.

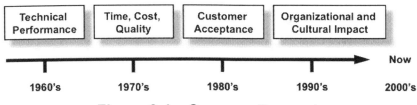

Figure 2.4 – Success Expansion

We can consider a hypothetical example of a CIA audio listening device to illustrate this expansion of the success definition. In the early days, success might have involved no more then getting the microphone and transmitter to work: technical performance. Then, when the triple constraint came into play, that audio listening device would have needed, not only to work, but also to have been developed on schedule and on budget. Subsequently, when the fourth dimension of customer acceptance was added to the success definition, that audio listening device would have had to collect audio intelligence of sufficient value as to satisfy the customer. And now, with another definition expansion, that audio listening device would not only be required to meet all of the previous criteria, but also to produce a lasting intelligence benefit. Today, this expanded success definition, including lasting organizational benefit, might compel an IT organization to gauge project success according to the level of new market penetration. For NASA, this type of success gauge was used by former President Bush[9] in 2004 when he declared that the United States chooses to explore space because doing so "improves our lives, and lifts our national spirit." The way I see it, lifting national spirit is a huge expansion in the definition of project success, one that I am certain can not be achieved without getting executives to act for project success.

More Complexity

Projects are more complex. So much so, that success through the actions of the individual project manager is increasingly rare. Projects are more interconnected, more interdependent, and more interrelated than ever before. So too are the businesses in which projects are being conducted; businesses now have complex alliances with strategic suppliers, networks of customers, and partnerships with allies and even with competitors. The result is that business systems are significantly more complex than in the past. Gone are the days where the typical project deliverable is a stand-alone product used by

	Duration	Cost	Scope	Team	Urgency	Flexibility	Volatility	Stakeholders
Small Independent Low Risk								
Medium Some Complexity Some Risk								
Large High Complexity High Risk								

Figure 2.5 – Complexity Assessment

a single customer; instead, systems are being delivered for stakeholder groups with divergent needs. Recognizing the increase in project complexity, PMI selected a book about managing complex projects as their 2009 Book of the Year.[10] Additionally, PMI also developed a publication titled *Navigating Complexity: A Practice Guide*,[11] that observes "globalization, new technologies, and fragmented supply chains have significantly increased and compounded the complexity of what practitioners are being asked to manage."

For an example of the evolving nature of project complexity, we can look at the information technology segment. IT systems have evolved through a series of complexity stages, beginning with mainframe computers, progressing to stand-alone workstations, and evolving into networked and enterprise systems that are commonplace today. Likewise for the hypothetical CIA audio listening device, a simple wired microphone might have evolved into a stand-alone audio transmitter, which might have evolved into a system of audio transmitters and controllers, which ultimately could have evolved into a global enterprise network of audio collection systems. The complexity level of a project can be appraised, as shown in Figure 2.5, by examining its dimensions, such as duration, cost, scope, project team size, schedule urgency, cost/duration/scope flexibility, requirements volatility, number of stakeholders.[12] An increasingly popular device for assessing complexity, the Cynefin framework,[13] offers five decision-making contexts or domains: simple, complicated, complex, chaotic, and disorder. That framework helps to make important distinctions between "known unknowns," where the relationship between cause and effect requires analysis or expertise, and "unknown unknowns," where cause and effect can only be deduced in retrospect.

In complex projects, where there is a preponderance of unknown unknowns, the project manager is confronted with the seemingly impossible task of "shooting in the dark" toward satisfying expectations that will only be known after the fact. I am certain that satisfying those expectations can not be achieved without getting executives to act for project success.

More Projects

Adding to the problem is the fact that there are many more projects and frequently not enough project managers. Best-selling business author Tom Peters[14] has stated that "all work is project work." Maybe that helps to put into context a recent worldwide PMI job growth report that states,[15] "there's a widening gap between employers' need for skilled project management workers and the availability of professionals to fill those roles." This talent gap is so large that $208 billion in GDP losses are projected during the next decade because of insufficient project management talent. This deficit will put tremendous pressure on the project managers who are in the workforce; the all-too-familiar "do more with less" approach is sure to accelerate.[16] Trying to do more with less will further drive up the need for executive actions if project success is going to be achieved.

Chapter Highlights

Project managers who continue doing what used to work by focusing within the bounds of the project are now finding success more difficult to achieve. The problem is that project success is dependent to an increased degree not only on the efforts of the project manager but also on the efforts of the executive as well. Unfortunately, about three-fourths of the project managers are not getting the levels of executive support they need.

For the purpose of conveying the concepts in this book, a broad definition has been adopted for the executive; it includes most anyone in the organization with more authority and power than the project manager.

The problem is compounded by the expanding definition of project success; it has evolved from the single dimension of technical performance to the point of including the triple constraint of time/cost/quality, customer acceptance, and organizational/cultural impact. Furthermore, project complexity has expanded. Gone are the days where the typical project deliverable is a stand-alone product used by a single customer; instead, systems are being delivered for groups of stakeholders with diverging needs. Additionally, the widening gap between employers' need for skilled project management workers and the availability of professionals to fill those roles is further intensifying the need for executive actions.

Chapter End Notes

[1] Towers Perrin. (2008). *Global workforce study.* Valhalla, NY: Towers Perrin. The study included over 30,000 responses. This company merged in 2016 to become Willis Towers Watson; they continue to produce annual global workforce studies.

[2] Council for Excellence in Government. (2008). Delivering program results. *The Public Manager 37(4).* Note that the report's use of the term "program manager" may be considered synonymous with the general usage of the term "project manager."

[3] PricewaterhouseCoopers. (2012). *Insights and trends: current portfolio, programme, and project management practices.* London, UK: PricewaterhouseCoopers. The study included 38 countries. Poor estimation during the planning phase was identified as the largest contributor to project failure; lack of executive sponsorship was second.

[4] This expansive view of responsibility, to include co-workers and the organization, is often referred to as transformational leadership where the focus is on changing the organizational culture. It differs from the transactional view of leadership where the focus is on working within the existing organizational culture.

[5] This reality can seem a bit harsh to some project managers who recognize that they are being held responsible for outcomes in which they do not have full authority.

[6] Schein, E. (2016). *Organizational culture and leadership (fifth edition)*. New York: John Wiley & Sons. The author is recognized as the 'father' of organizational culture, world-renowned for his expertise and research in the field; in this book, he analyzes and illustrates through cases the abstract concept of culture and shows its importance to the management of organizational change. I long ago adopted the perspective that, as a leader, it was my primary job to shape the workplace culture.

[7] The Standish Group. (2013). *Chaos report 2013*. West Yarmouth, MA: The Standish Group. The project failure and challenged rates identified in this report pertain to the Information Technology sector. These rates have remained above 62% during the past two decades. Rates for other sectors are comparable.

[8] Archibald, R. (2003). *Managing high-technology programs & projects (third edition)*. Hoboken, NJ: John Wiley & Sons. This book edition included information about the organizational culture in which the project resides, a topic absent from earlier editions. Russell Archibald is an original founding trustee and member of the Project Management Institute.

[9] Bush, G. (2004). President Bush announces new vision for space program exploration. *The White House*. Retrieved January 22, 2018, from https://history.nasa.gov/Bush%20SEP.htm. This speech followed the national disaster in 2003 of the Columbia Shuttle when all seven crew members were killed.

[10] Hass, K. (2008). *Managing complex projects: a new model*. Tysons Corner, VA: Management Concepts. Dimensions of project complexity have been defined and plotted on a spider diagram.

[11] Project Management Institute. (2014). *Navigating complexity: a practice guide*. Newtown Square, PA: Project Management Institute. The guide identified three categories of complexity: human behavior, system behavior, and ambiguity.

[12] While this increased level of project complexity can be quite disconcerting for many project managers, I personally find it quite similar to the high tech, high risk, one-of-a-kind development environment I spent decades working in at the CIA.

[13] Snowden, D., & Boone, M. (November 2007). A leader's framework for decision making. *Harvard Business Review.* Retrieved January 22, 2018, from https://hbr.org/2007/11/a-leaders-framework-for-decision-making. The Cynefin is a conceptual framework used to help managers, decision makers, and others reach decisions.

[14] Peters, T. (2006). *In search of excellence: lessons from america's best-run companies (reprint edition).* New York City, NY: Harper Business. This book captured powerfully effective insights into what contributes to making a company excellent.

[15] Project Management Institute. (2017). *Job growth and talent gap 2017-2027.* Newtown Square, PA: Project Management Institute. The reported talent gap has widened since the earlier 2008 and 2012 reports.

[16] One very public example of the limits of trying to do more with less occurred in the early 1990's at NASA when then NASA Administrator Dan Goldin directed the agency to adopt the faster, better, cheaper approach to project management of its space and earth science missions. The goal was to shorten development times, reduce cost, and increase the scientific return by flying more missions in less time. Although there were some successes that occurred using this approach, the *NASA Faster Better Cheaper Final Report* found that it resulted in driving up the mission failure rate to unacceptable levels. Retrieved January 22, 2018, from https://mars.nasa.gov/msp98/misc/fbctask.pdf.

Chapter 3

IDENTIFY EXECUTIVE ACTIONS

"Some people succeed by what they know, some by what they do, and a few by what they are."

Elbert Hubbard 1856-1915
American writer

Much Known

The good news associated with the topic of executive actions for project success is that a number of experienced project managers and authors have been articulate about the actions that they would like executives to take. Robert Graham and Randall Englund[1] wrote about creating the project environment, Harold Kerzner[2] wrote about excellence in project management, Gary Heerkens[3] wrote about implementing project management in any organization, James Schneidmuller and Judy Balaban[4] wrote about creating a project management center of excellence, Rick Mauer[5] wrote about moving beyond the wall of resistance, and the Project Management Institute[6] published a guide to best practices of project management groups in large functional organizations. More recently, a book by Randall Englund and Alfonso Bucero[7] addressed achieving management commitment through sponsorship, and research by Timothy Kloppenborg[8] has emerged about the sponsor's role in the various project phases. Furthermore, for the first time ever, an entire section in *The PMBOK® Guide* addresses the project environment.[9]

We can add to these publications the voices of many experienced project managers. These are individuals who have moved beyond success managing relatively low complexity and low risk projects to struggling toward success managing more complex and higher risk projects. These experienced project managers are the "Georges and Georgettes" who had been looking at their executives as contributors to the problem and would now prefer to look at their executives as people with whom they can build a strong mutual partnership, as suggested in Figure 3.1, to take actions for project success. As a consequence of writing and speaking extensively on this subject and as a result of the consulting I have undertaken in this subject area, I have benefited from a significant number of direct interactions with project managers and with executives. Most of these interactions were with people who responded thoughtfully and provided their recommended executive actions for project success. The publications cited, the interactions with project managers and executives, and my assessments form the basis for the list of executive actions in this book as shown in Figure 3.2. This list can be used to help move projects, project managers, and the organization toward more success more of the time. This list can also be used by project managers to help guide the development of a strong mutual partnership with their executive.

Figure 3.1 – Dear Executive

By all means, read these publications and others, consider the executive actions list in this book, and then make a list for yourself. You can build on the solid basis for the list in this book by blending your experience and your judgment, by reflecting upon the unique circumstances of your project and organization, by soliciting from your fellow project managers, and by tempering the list with the reality of what can be achieved in your situation.

Organize And Manage Work As Projects

At the top of the list of executive actions is organizing the work into projects. Project managers can feel like fish out of water when they work in an environment that is not structured around projects. There is a strong preference for sectioning off the non-project work to other organizational elements and people. In a non-project environment much effort can be spent trying to educate and convince the myriad stakeholders about the merits of the project process basics. Discussions and disagreements can repeatedly occur about the amount of planning, the completeness of requirements definition, the use of baselines and change management, schedule precision, and the criteria for accepting a project deliverable. Most certainly, these can be productive discussions. However, each time they occur, they draw time and resources away from the actual management of the projects. Importantly, they limit the odds of project success. Study findings in a recent *PMI Pulse of the Profession* report[10] indicate that projects are 2.5 times more successful when repeatable project management practices are used. It is far more efficient to have these discussions once, to establish and document a standardized project management process, and to be accountable for following that process. Then, over time, as the project managers and the executives gain experience with the standardized process, it can be suitably tailored for each individual project, and it can be incrementally improved.

WHAT TO DO

☐ **Organize And Manage Work As Projects**

☐ **Pick The Right Projects**

☐ **Maintain Close Stakeholder Relationships**

☐ **Use Suitable Project Management Process**

☐ **Ensure Projects Follow Documented Plan**

☐ **Ensure Projects Are Based On Requirements**

☐ **Ensure Resources Are Sufficient**

☐ **Engage Middle Management Help**

☐ **Use Job Performance Standards**

☐ **Make And Support Timely Decisions**

☐ **Ask The Right Questions**

Figure 3.2 – Executive Actions List

In project-based organizations and organizational elements, each project benefits from having a designated project manager and from having a designated sponsor. Here, the project manager is delegated adequate authority to establish a baseline, to manage the project according to that baseline, and to hold the sponsor and others accountable for supporting that baseline. Note that when this authority is delegated by the executive to the project manager, the project manager understands that responsibility and accountability are expected in return.[11]

Pick The Right Projects

Picking the right projects can be as sophisticated as strategic portfolio management or as simple as doing only those projects for which the project managers and project teams have the capacity. Either way, the goal is to identify a limited number of top-priority projects. I had the good fortune, as a CIA employee, of working in an organization that not only was an early adopter of project management, but also an early adopter of portfolio management.[12] Now, an entire practice area has formed around picking the right projects; it has matured to the point where PMI has published *The Standard for Portfolio Management*.[13] Consider this reality: when too many projects are considered the number one priority, in reality none of them is. I favor the simple approach: do only as many projects as can be done well, and do not agonize too much over the decisions about which projects to undertake. Do not overtask the project manager. Actual research into the optimum number of projects for a project manager to manage successfully is sparse; however, the few works that I have come across do coincide with empirical evidence. Fewer projects are better; fewer projects mean more time spent per project. Although counterintuitive for some, fewer projects mean that ultimately more projects conclude successfully. Additionally, since successful projects do not overrun budgets or schedules, money and time become available for other projects.

Picking the right projects also involves assessing the fit between the nature of the project and the abilities of the project manager. For example, a history of managing information technology projects successfully does not necessarily indicate a strong aptitude for managing CIA audio listening device projects. Recent research into project manager assignments has reflected the expanded project success definition and the increase in project complexity now to include a strategic aspect of project manager assignment.[14] A good fit not only raises the odds of the project being successful, but it also raises the odds of the project manager being successful.[15]

Maintain Close Stakeholder Relationships

Executives have a unique opportunity to develop and maintain close stakeholder and customer relationships that complement and enhance the relationships formed by the project manager. The time invariably comes when an issue, concern, or decision needs to be addressed by someone other than the project manager. Project funding, priority, and requirements are often topics that benefit from this type of supportive intervention. Note that these executive relationships should be conducted so that the project manager's authority and responsibility are maintained and so that the project manager is kept in the loop and well informed. Ideally, it is the project manager who is serving up the topics for the executive to use as the basis for the stakeholder and customer relationships.

The value of executive relationships with stakeholders has received considerably more attention recently. The latest edition of *The Standard For Program Management*[16] describes the value of relationships with the sponsor, steering committee, program manager, program management office, funding organization, customers, suppliers, and regulatory agencies. It also describes, in broad terms, the value of relationships with other groups, including political, legal, human resources, consumer, environmental, administration, and infrastructure. The value of these executive relationships with stakeholders has been further reinforced in PMI's recent publication titled *Navigating Complexity: A Practice Guide*,[17] with the observation that "executives with strong leadership skills play a key role in enabling successful program and project outcomes."

Use Suitable Project Management Process

Project management is a discipline and, as such, benefits from adhering to a suitable project management process. Project managers who are at the top of their game have come to rely on executives to establish a standardized process for their organization to use. They seek to be held accountable for applying tailored versions of this process to each of their projects. In the absence of executive action, they can develop and follow their own processes, but they recognize the limits in efficiency and effectiveness in doing so. For project managers, there is freedom through suitable process. According to a recent *PMI Pulse of the Profession* report, for organizations, the use of a suitable standard process increases project success rates by 23%.[18]

Ideally, the standardized process has been developed to reflect both the nature of the work being addressed by the projects and the experience level of the project managers. As with the Goldilocks principle, there should not be too much process, and there should not be too little; it should be just right as illustrated in Figure 3.3. It is worth noting, with perhaps a bit of humor, that even Attila the Hun used a suitable project management process. Pillage then burn because it did not work the other way around. Over time, as both the organization and the project managers gain more experience and mature, the standard process can be adjusted accordingly. In this way, the process remains suitable.

Georgette worked in the operations element of an organization that was dedicated to reacting quickly to tasking from overseas; speed was key. Nevertheless, when she was confronted with a task to develop a set of special electronic beacons and ship them within 48 hours, she had the wherewithal to dedicate half of that time to requirements analysis, planning, and design; the fabrication occurred during the second half. Her 48-hour project was successful largely because she used a suitable project management process. For that, she received a project management of the year award.

Figure 3.3 – Process Story

Ensure Projects Follow Documented Plan

Project managers expect executives to ensure that they follow a documented project plan. They expect to be given adequate time up front during the initial project phase to build this baseline document and to be isolated from pressure to proceed hastily without it; they also expect to be held accountable for continuous controlled revisions to the plan throughout the project life cycle. This expectation applies not only for predictive life cycles (such as waterfall), but also for iterative, incremental, and adaptive (such as agile) life cycles. As John Stenbeck, best-selling author of the *Agile Almanac*,[19] opines when he finds planning lacking in agile, "that is not agile, that is agile as an excuse for bad behavior." Planning is the foundation for project management, and as such, its level of importance cannot be overstated. Virtually every set of project performance statistics I have examined during the past couple of decades lists inadequate planning as a leading cause, if not the leading cause, of project failure. For example, in a recent global survey by PricewaterhouseCoopers of over 200 organizations conducting business in a broad array of sectors, bad planning and estimating was identified as the primary cause of failure.[20]

Determining the scope of a project is difficult without spending a considerable amount of up-front time properly planning. Gathering requirements, developing comprehensive project management plans, assembling adequate resources, and determining and scheduling activities require considerable thought, coordination and, yes, a great deal of time. I advocate for using a suitable standardized project management process that includes sufficient time at the beginning for these activities. This up-front time is identified as "study period" in the version of the project life cycle included in one of the most popular project management books published.[21]

Without planning activities, these key project elements can lead to lack of stakeholder commitment and resources because poor planning does not instill confidence or credibility. In turn, this lack has the potential to discourage stakeholders from proceeding with the project manager or even with a project altogether. Project managers instill confidence by keeping on top of project planning activities, and therefore, reduce the need for costly, time-consuming rework to increase project success rates organization-wide.

Figure 3.4 – Planning

The benefits of planning have been captured with the military adage, as represented in Figure 3.4, "proper prior planning prevents particularly poor performance." Other versions of this adage, sometimes colorful, have also been used; as have various other related sayings as well.[22] And, as in the military, many organizations celebrate heroics, success through individual efforts overcoming the odds. I very much support recognizing individual project managers for their outstanding achievements, courage, and noble qualities. However, in the context of project management, I much prefer to be a hero with a plan. To put it another way, if there is no planning, there is no project, and there is no need for a project manager, at least not the kind of project manager I have spent a career aspiring to become.

Ensure Projects Are Based On Requirements

Requirements are at the core of successful project management. Together with planning, according to a recent *PMI Pulse of the Profession* report, requirements top the list of leading causes of project failure.[23] Because requirements are so important, they play essential roles in two project management related disciplines as well, systems engineering[24] and business analysis.[25] Both of these disciplines include mature processes and practices for the management of requirements; elements from these disciplines were folded into CIA's Project Management Training and Certification program and the U.S. Federal Acquisition Certification for Program and Project Managers.[26]

Project managers expect executives to ensure that they base projects on requirements. They expect to be given adequate time up front during the initial project phase to establish the requirements, perform adequate requirements analysis, build this baseline document, and be isolated from pressure to proceed hastily without it; they also expect to be held accountable for continuous controlled revisions to the requirements throughout the project life cycle. Project managers understand that the nature of the requirements plays a central role in the selection of an appropriate project life cycle; choices include versions of predictive (such as waterfall), iterative, incremental, and adaptive (such as agile) life cycles. They understand that the timing and formatting of the requirements is dependent on that life cycle selection, earlier and more formal for predictive life cycles and less formal and later for adaptive life cycles.[27] Additionally, project managers understand that omissions and inaccuracies early in the requirements process have a huge multiplying effect on the overall project cost. This cost escalation has been studied in a number of industries, including the space program; a NASA study found that the cost of fixing a requirements error was about 1,000 times greater during the operations phase than during the up-front requirements phase.[28]

George, the project manager responsible for the development of a large new data processing center, established a mandatory data retrieval speed requirement with which interested vendors had to comply. As the contract was about to be awarded to the only bidder compliant with this mandatory requirement, it was discovered that they proposed an unconventional approach. Instead of the expected information technology network-attached system, the vendor intended to use a room full of physical file drawers and a staff of athletic runners.

Figure 3.5 – Requirement Story

Without an adequate understanding of the requirements, the estimations of scope, schedule, and risk will invariably be inaccurate. Thus, the mechanism for determining customer satisfaction will less likely be based on the actual project deliverable performance as illustrated in Figure 3.5. The way I look at it, a well-understood requirement is a requirement half solved.

Ensure Resources Are Sufficient

Project managers look to their executives to ensure that project resources (time, people, and money) are commensurate with needs. If shortages and/or changes occur, the executive should expect to receive an impact assessment from the project manager that has been developed in an environment without excessive pressure to absorb the change or simplistically do more with less. This impact assessment, which could serve as the basis for plan revisions, would be formulated with respect to the plans, requirements, and other documents that have been baselined. I have found that I can gain a significant amount of insight into executives by their reactions, when they are asking me to do more with less, when I respond by saying, "I will let you know the impact." This simple direct statement touches on the division of responsibility between the project manager and executive, it touches on the legitimacy of the already baselined project plan and requirements documents, and it touches on the project manager and executive relationship.

If you are like me, and I know I am, then you have developed a certain level of competency as a project manager, not necessarily as a finance manager, controller, chief financial officer, or any other financial profession. Certainly, as part of my project management responsibilities, I developed competence in budgeting and estimating, in developing work packages, and in other areas related to the development and management of budgets. However, that does not translate into an ability, or even an interest, in securing funding and other resources. That task, I feel, is better left up to professionals in those fields.

Engage Middle Management Help

Figure 3.6 – Middle

Engaging middle management can be a powerful bottom-up and top-down step executives can take toward project success as illustrated in Figure 3.6.

Since middle managers are closer to the projects and project managers than the executives are, they have the opportunity for a significant amount of bottom-up insight into the needs of those projects and project managers. Thanks to a study of middle managers in project management,[29] it is now understood that middle managers in successful organizations have their fingers on the resource needs of each of the projects within their portion of the organization, they have insight into the common issues impacting those projects, and they have the opportunity to spot common emerging project-related hot spots and trends. Consequently, middle managers are particularly well positioned to reflect on the common project and project manager needs and sort through the list of possible executive actions to prioritize those with the most potential for positive impact.

Furthermore, when the time comes, middle managers are also well positioned to help tailor and implement the top-down actions from executives. According to a *Harvard Business Review* report, they actually have more influence over the success of those implementations than any other element in the organization.[30] In those cases, middle managers are not only able to implement the actions, but also actually able to lead them by working the levers of power up, across, and down in their organizations.

It is worth noting the significant step that was taken a decade ago in understanding the role of middle managers, when the first program management standard was published.[31] That standard describes a number of roles and responsibilities related to project success suitable for middle managers, including governance, strategy alignment, benefits management, life cycle management, and stakeholder engagement.

Use Job Performance Standards

Project managers, especially those who are in it for the long term, are interested in working in an established career path with established job standards. Russell Archibald, PMI founding member number six, states that project managers view project management as highly personal, as a way of life, as a way of making a living, and as a challenge of their capabilities that can provide deep satisfaction.[32] These project managers understand that the outcome of their projects plays a significant role in their career advancement, and they understand the value of being evaluated against a common set of competency-based job performance standards. According to a recent talent management study, organizations using established job standards experience a substantial increase in project success rates.[33] However, since according to a recent *PMI Pulse of the Profession* report, fewer than half of today's organizations have a formal process for developing project manager competence or a defined career path for project managers,[34] success for projects and project managers is being stifled.

Incidental, accidental, part-time, and interim project managers can benefit from job performance standards as well. These project managers are individuals who may be employing, or trying to employ, project management practices even though they may not be in full-time, established project manager positions. The project management practices may be incidental to the primary focus of their job, or they may find themselves performing these practices quite by accident without the realization that the practices are associated with project management, or they may look at their practice of project management as a temporary assignment.

Valuable information is now available for those organizations looking to establish job performance standards. A recently released competency framework from PMI includes an extensive set of defined knowledge, performance, and personal competencies.[35] Additionally, the U.S. federal government has developed a set of project management competencies.[36] These competency sets, which address leadership as well as project management, can be used as the basis for the development of job performance standards and career paths.

Make And Support Timely Decisions

Successful project managers have learned the benefits of identifying and managing against the critical path, the sequence of project activities that determine the shortest completion time. Any delay, for whatever reason, in the critical path will delay project completion and/or negatively impact the project cost and scope. Consequently, project managers are looking to their executives to make the timely decisions needed to stay on the critical path.

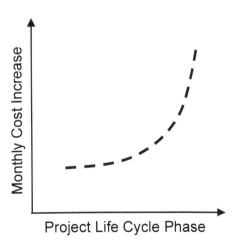

Figure 3.7 – Delay Cost

According to Don Reinersten, father of the Cost of Delay concept, the cost of delay and disruption has evolved into a mature discipline capable of accurately identifying the contributors to and costs of delay.[37] According to a recent paper in *PM World Journal*, these delays, depending on the life cycle phase of the project and other factors, can easily add a significant amount to the total cost for each month of delay as illustrated in Figure 3.7.[38] The situation becomes even more costly in situations where the delay impacts the time to market or, worse, when market launch windows are missed entirely. A recent study by PMI found that almost half of all failed projects were impacted by poor decision making.[39]

I have come to understand that when an important decision is required of an executive, it is my responsibility as project manager to provide the necessary information upon which that decision can be made. This includes alternatives, recommendations, risks, and a basis that is expressed in the business terms important to the executive. I will let the executive know the impact of each alternative being considered. For example, if the decision involved a hypothetical CIA listening device, I would express the impact not only in terms of the schedule, but also in terms of the risk of missing the opportunity to collect important intelligence.

Once the decision is made by the executive, project managers are looking for that decision to be supported actively and visibly by the executive. That support may include additional time, additional resources, or additional commitments from stakeholders.

Ask The Right Questions

This is my favorite executive action for project success. It speaks to the strong mutual partnership that is central to getting the executive to act for project success. It also speaks to the difference between the roles and responsibilities of the executive and the project manager. Asking the right questions can help the executive minimize the tempting distraction to get too far into the project details, to solve the project issues, to get ahead of themselves or the schedule, or to encroach on doing the project manager's job as represented in Figure 3.8. Asking the right questions can serve as a starting point and/or reinforcement for executives who are looking to

> Georgette was discouraged by the project review she conducted with the steering committee. Although the project had just begun, she was being asked detailed design questions which she could not answer. She tried unsuccessfully to deflect these questions by pointing out the project was in the requirements definition phase and had not yet reached the design phase. It seemed as if the members of the steering committee were very disappointed in her performance because she could not provide detailed technical answers to their questions.

Figure 3.8 – Roles Story

behave in a manner that demonstrates their support for project managers, and it can uncover actions the executive can take for project success.

With considerable input from executives and project managers, I compiled a list of the right questions for the executive to ask as shown in Figure 3.9.

Years ago when I first provided this list of questions to an executive who had several hundred project managers in his organization, I was impressed by what he did with the list. He reduced the physical size of the list and affixed it to the back of his employee badge that he wore on a lanyard around his neck; that way he could unobtrusively glance at it when engaging in a discussion with a project manager. Ever since that experience, I have provided the list pre-sized for that very purpose.

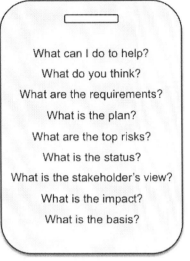

What can I do to help?

What do you think?

What are the requirements?

What is the plan?

What are the top risks?

What is the status?

What is the stakeholder's view?

What is the impact?

What is the basis?

Figure 3.9 – Questions

At the top of the list is perhaps the most effective question for the executive to ask the project manager, "What can I do to help?" The effectiveness of this question has repeatedly been demonstrated during the forty years since it was first associated with the groundbreaking servant leadership approach by Robert Greenleaf into the nature of power and greatness.[40] It places the executive in a position to support the project manager while at the same time holding him or her accountable for responsibilities and commitments. A favorite true story of mine from history, which was captured in a fascinating leadership book, illustrates this approach; the story took place a century ago when Ernest Shackleton, captain of the ship "Endurance," was dealing with the consequences of being stranded for over a year with no hope of rescue after the ship had been crushed by Antarctic ice.[41] On a daily basis under the extreme cold and seemingly hopeless conditions, Shackleton would engage each of the two dozen men in the ship's crew in a one-on-one conversation centered on their assigned duties for that day. During each of those personal interactions, he would reinforce the expectation for successful completion of the assigned duty by the crew member, and he would ask what he could do to help. Under the extreme and life-threatening conditions, the asking of that question not only increased the odds of successful completion of the duty, but it also changed the nature of the relationship between the captain and crew member; it moved from a "me vs. you" to a "we" type of relationship, as in "we are in this together." This served to boost morale to the point of further contributing to success. Because of this servant leader relationship, several of the men wrote in their journals that in spite of the extreme hardship, "this was the best time of their lives."

This "What can I do to help?" approach that is embodied in servant leadership has become increasingly popular because it works. One-third of *Fortune Magazine's* "100 Best Companies to Work For" practice the principles of servant leadership, and that percentage seems to be growing.[42] Unlike leadership approaches with a top-down hierarchical style, in servant leadership, the leader is a servant first. Servant leaders understand that they must meet the needs of their followers in order to enable them to reach their full potential. Servant leaders strive to respect and to motivate their followers, using their influence to inspire followers to reach new heights. They lead from behind using empathetic listening skills, employing persuasion, and building community within the project team. Servant leaders are individuals of character, put people first, are skilled communicators, are compassionate collaborators, are systems thinkers, and exercise moral authority.[43]

The "What do you think?" question honors the position the project manager is in to know substantially more than others about his or her project. The "What are the requirements?" and "What is the plan?" questions speak to the practice of establishing baselines upon which comparisons can be made. Those comparisons can take the form of the "What are the top risks?" and "What is the status?" questions when they are asked in the form of "compared to plan." Referencing questions to the baselined plan reinforces the nature of the agreement represented by those documents. Both the executive and the project manager have agreed that unless a change is negotiated, tasks and activities will proceed according to those documents. Conversely, those agreements signify that there will not be any expectations to proceed in any manner that deviates from those documents.

Asking "What is the stakeholder's view?" positively reinforces the mutual responsibilities of both the project manager and executive to remain abreast of the views of all of the various stakeholders. Since project change is inevitable, asking "What is the impact?" of changes under consideration, when asked in the form of "compared to plan," further reinforces the value of managing against an established baseline. And finally, asking "What is the basis?" provides the opportunity for the project manager to demonstrate a high level of professionalism by supporting his or her opinions with substantive reasoning.

When taken together, these questions reinforce the strong mutual partnership between the project manager and the executive.

Chapter Highlights

Much is already known about the actions project managers would like their executives to take for project success. The well-researched executive actions list in this book can be tailored and used to address the reality of what can be achieved in your specific organization. Executive actions listed in this book include the following:

- Organize and manage work as projects
- Pick the right projects
- Maintain close stakeholder relationships
- Use suitable project management process
- Ensure projects follow documented plan
- Ensure projects are based on requirements
- Ensure resources are sufficient
- Engage middle management help
- Use job performance standards
- Make and support timely decisions
- Ask the right questions

Chapter End Notes

[1] Graham, R., & Englund, R. (1997). *Creating an environment for successful projects*. San Francisco, CA: Jossey-Bass. A second edition of this book was also published. Randall Englund, together with co-author Alfonso Bucero, published a follow-on book in 2012 titled *The Complete Project Manager: Integrating People, Organizational, and Technical Skills*.

[2] Kerzner, H. (1998). *In search of excellence in project management.* New York, NY: Van Nostrand Reinhold. Harold Kerzner has been one of the best-selling project management authors. His *Project Management: A Systems Approach to Planning, Scheduling and Controlling* book has become a de-facto standard in project management classes and on reference shelves; it is now in its twelfth edition.

[3] Heerkens, G. (2000*). How to implement project management in any organization*. PMI Annual Seminars & Symposium 2000. Houston, TX. This paper included a list of five essential ingredients to establish a project management culture.

[4] Schneidmuller, J., & Balaban, J. (2000). *From project management council to center of excellence: the journey continues…"* PMI Annual Seminars & Symposium 2000. Houston, TX. The authors described the successful establishment of a project management culture at AT&T.

[5] Mauer, R. (2010). *Beyond the wall of resistance: why 70% of all changes still fail – and what you can do about it (second edition).* Austin, TX: Bard Books Inc. The author provided insight in change management techniques.

[6] Project Management Institute (1997). *Best practices of project management groups in large functional organizations.* Newtown Square, PA: Project Management Institute. This research report included the results of a Fortune 500 project management benchmarking study.

[7] Englund, R., & Bucero, A. (2015). *Project sponsorship (second edition).* San Francisco, CA: Jossey-Bass. The authors advocated for a formally established project sponsor role.

[8] Kloppenborg, T., Tesch, D., & Manolis, C. (2014, February/March). Project success and executive sponsor behaviors: empirical life cycle stage investigations. *Project Management Journal.* Newtown Square, PA: Project Management Institute. The research findings suggested that during the executing stage, project sponsors should focus on ensuring communications as a top priority.

[9] Project Management Institute. (2017). *A guide to the project management body of knowledge (PMBOK®) (sixth edition).* Newtown Square, PA: Project Management Institute. This edition included a new 9-page section focused on the environment in which projects operate that listed internal and external factors that can impact the project. The publication also included an updated treatment of stakeholder management that first appeared in the previous edition.

[10] Project Management Institute. (2016). *Pulse of the profession: the high cost of low performance.* Newtown Square, PA: Project Management Institute. This global survey publication findings showed that when organizations embrace repeatable project, program, and portfolio management practices, they have better outcomes.

[11] Organizing and managing work as projects does not have to be an "all or nothing" situation. Organizational elements and/or pockets within organizational elements can be configured in this manner. Such a hybrid structure recognizes that while some work may be project work, other work may be ongoing operations or production.

[12] O'Brochta, M. (2001, November). *Opportunity assessment: before it is a project.* PMI Annual Seminars & Symposium 2001. Nashville, Tennessee. The author led the CIA effort to develop a standardized project life cycle methodology that included an opportunity assessment phase.

[13] Project Management Institute. (2017). *The standard for portfolio management (fourth edition)*. Newtown Square, PA: Project Management Institute. Considerable attention was given to a process that supports the organization's long-term strategic vision, including the organization's capability.

[14] Patanakul, P. (2015). Project manager assignment: a strategic perspective. *Open Economics and Management Journal 2015(2) Supplement 1: M4,* 21-28. Erie, PA: The Pennsylvania State University. The research findings included a process and set of strategic criteria for project manager assignment.

[15] I advocate for project managers, where possible, to have a significant say in the assignment of projects. In this way, they can, in a meaningful and personal way, evaluate the likelihood of their own ability to succeed.

[16] Project Management Institute. (2017). *The standard for program management (fourth edition)*. Newtown Square, PA: Project Management Institute. Considerable attention was given to the responsibility of managing the benefits that the project is expected to produce.

[17] Project Management Institute. (2014). *Navigating complexity: a practice guide*. Newtown Square, PA: Project Management Institute. The guide identified, in multiple places, the responsibility for the executive actively to provide support. Three categories of complexity were listed: human behavior, system behavior, and ambiguity.

[18] Project Management Institute. (2015). *Pulse of the profession: capturing the value of project management*. Newtown Square, PA: Project Management Institute. The report stated that organizations with standardized project management practices have a 73% project success rate compared to a 50% project success rate in organizations without standardized project management practices.

[19] Stenbeck, J. (2015). *Agile almanac: book 1: single-team projects & exam book*. Spokane, WA: GR8PM Inc. This book shot to the top of the charts soon after release; it has been followed *by Agile Almanac: Book 2: Programs with Multi and Virtual Team Environments*.

[20] PricewaterhouseCoopers. (2012). *Insights and trends: current portfolio, programme, and project management practices*. London, UK: PricewaterhouseCoopers. The study included 38 countries. Poor estimation during the planning phase was identified as the largest contributor to project failure; lack of executive sponsorship was second.

[21] Foresberg, K., Mooz, H., & Cotterman, H. (1996). *Visualizing project management: models and frameworks for mastering complex systems.* Hoboken, NJ: John Wiley & Sons. Versions of this book's project life cycle and Vee model have been widely adopted by many organizations including NSA, CIA, and INCOSE. Second and third editions of this book that expand on these models have been published.

[22] Some of my favorite planning-related sayings are as follows: Failing to plan is planning to fail; Not planning has the benefit of avoiding the anxiety that precedes certain failure; A goal without a plan is just a wish; Bad planning on your part does not constitute an emergency on my part; Plan your work and work your plan.

[23] Project Management Institute. (2014). *Pulse of the profession: requirements management.* Newtown Square, PA: Project Management Institute. The report stated that poor requirements management was the second most common reason for project failure. 87% of organizations surveyed recognized that improvement is needed. Only 49% of organizations had the resources in place to do requirements management properly. Only one-third of organizations' leaders valued requirements management as a critical competency. Only 47% of organizations had a formal process to validate requirements. 51% of project and program dollars were wasted due to poor requirements management. 47% of unmet project goals were due to poor requirements management.

[24] The Systems Engineering Body of Knowledge (SEBoK) is developed and produced by the joint efforts of the International Council on Systems Engineering (INCOSE), Institute of Electrical and Electronics Engineers (IEEE) Computer Society, and the Systems Engineering Research Center. SEBoK version 1.9 was released on 30 November 2017.

[25] The Guide to the Business Analysis Body of Knowledge (BABOK Guide) is developed by the International Institute of Business Analysis. BABOK version 3 was released in 2015.

[26] O'Brochta, M. (2004). *Project management certification now underway at the CIA.* PMI Global Congress Proceedings 2004. Anaheim, California. The author led the CIA effort to develop and implement their Project Management Training and Certification Program, and he helped develop and implement the U.S. Government's Federal Acquisition Certification for Program and Project Managers.

[27] One useful treatment of the requirements life cycle has been included in the BABOK: stated, confirmed, communicated, traced, approved, maintained, prioritized, analyzed, verified, validated, and allocated.

[28] Stecklein, J. (2004, June). *Error cost escalation through the project life cycle.* INCOSE 14th Annual International Symposium 2004. Toulouse, France. The rate of cost escalation was found to rise at an exponential rate through the life cycle.

[29] Blomquist, T., & Muller, R. (2006). *Middle managers in program and portfolio management: practices, roles and responsibilities.* Newtown Square, PA: Project Management Institute. This work was one of a very few studies of the role of middle managers in project management.

[30] Tabrizi, B. (2014). The key to change is middle management. *Harvard Business Review.* Retrieved January 22, 2018, from https://hbr.org/2014/10/the-key-to-change-is-middle-management. This study included 56 randomly selected companies and interviews with 380 executives.

[31] Project Management Institute. (2017). *The standard for program management (fourth edition).* Newtown Square, PA: Project Management Institute. Understanding the value of middle managers in helping executives act for project success was accelerated when the first edition in 2006 of this standard was published; that edition, as do all subsequent editions, describes roles and responsibilities suitable for middle managers.

[32] Archibald, R. (2003). *Managing high-technology programs & projects (third edition).* Hoboken, NJ: John Wiley & Sons. Differing views of project management were included for top managers, functional managers, and project managers.

[33] Project Management Institute. (2014). *Talent management.* Newtown Square, PA: Project Management Institute. The report found that organizations with a defined career path, that develop project management competency, and that have ongoing training for staff on the use of project management tools and techniques are 12-13% more successful with their strategic initiatives than organizations that do not.

[34] Project Management Institute. (2017). *Pulse of the profession: success rates rise.* Newtown Square, PA: Project Management Institute. This global survey publication reported that 45% of the organization surveyed had a formal process in place for developing project manager competence, and 43% had a defined project management career path.

[35] Project Management Institute. (2017). *Project manager competency development framework (third edition).* Newtown Square, PA: Project Management Institute. This extensive document defined competencies for entry, mid, and senior level project managers.

[36] Federal Acquisition Institute. (2013). *Federal acquisition certification for program and project managers competency model*. Retrieved January 22, 2018, from https://www.fai.gov/drupal/sites/default/files/2013-9-23-PPM-Competency-Model.pdf. This extensive document provided a framework for the definition, assessment, and development of portfolio/program/project manager competency.

[37] Reinersten, D. (2009). *The principles of product development flow: second generation lean product development*. Redondo Beach, CA: Celeritas Publishing. The author first introduced the ideas that have now become known as lean product development.

[38] Prieto, B. (2014, February). Perspective on the cost of delayed decision making in large project execution. *PM World Journal*. Addison, TX: PM World Inc. This paper examined the cost of delay as a function of a wide variety of factors; it found that delays can easily add 1-5% to the total cost for each month of delay.

[39] Project Management Institute. (2015). *Capturing the value of project management through decision making*. Newtown Square, PA: Project Management Institute. This study found that effective decision making resulted in 79% more projects meeting original goals and business intent, 110% more projects were completed within budget, and 128% more were completed on time.

[40] Greenleaf, R., & Covey, S. (2002). *Servant leadership: a journey into the nature of legitimate power and greatness (25th anniversary edition)*. Mahwah, NJ: Paulist Press. First published in 1977, this groundbreaking book coined the term servant leadership and started a management theory movement that is embraced by many leading organizations. I was first introduced to servant leadership while listening to a riveting conference keynote a few years after this book was published. Since that introduction dovetailed with an early management assignment, I was open to trying the concept. It began working immediately, and I have faithfully tried to practice servant leadership ever since.

[41] Morrell, M., & Capparell, S. (2001). *Shackleton's way: leadership lessons from the great antarctic explorer*. New York, NY: Penguin Books. This book, which contained an analysis of the true and dramatic story of the Antarctic expedition led by Ernest Shackleton, cataloged a number of effective leadership techniques, including servant leadership.

[42] Hunter, J. (2004). *The world's most powerful leadership principle*. New York, NY: Random House. This book reported that 35 of the *Fortune* Magazine "100 Best Companies to Work For" identified servant leadership as a core principle. More recently, an analysis by the founder of ModernServantLeader.com found that five of the top ten companies on the Fortune 100 list practiced servant leadership. Retrieved January 22, 2018, from https://www.modernservantleader.com/servant-leadership/fortunes-best-companies-to-work-for-with-servant-leadership.

[43] Sipe, J., & Frick, D. (2015). *Seven pillars of servant leadership: practicing the wisdom of leading by serving (revised and expanded edition)*. Mahwah, NJ: Paulist Press. This book trained readers in how to evolve and implement the competencies and behaviors of servant leadership.

Chapter 4

IDENTIFY BARRIERS

"Knowledge is knowing a fact. Wisdom is knowing what to do with that fact."
B. J. Palmer 1881-1961
Developed chiropractic profession

Executive Limitations

Even the most progressive executives who are interested in supporting project managers by acting for project success often find that easier said than done. The demands of their executive responsibilities, the constraints they encounter both real and imagined, and their limited understanding of the discipline of project management hinder even the most enthusiastic among them as illustrated in Figure 4.1. It is essential for project managers who want to get their executives to act for project success to understand the barriers that their executives face. Only after gaining this insight can a project manager understand how effectively to help get their executive to take the actions necessary for project success.

George had politely lamented that the amount of supplemental funding his executive had just secured for his project was inadequate. He was unprepared for his executive's sudden and harsh response, "You do not know what I had to go through to get even that much." At that point George barked, "Maybe not, but you do not understand how impossible project success is with such an inadequate amount."

Figure 4.1 – Understand Story

Viewpoints Differ

The executive's viewpoint differs from that of the project manager. Notable project management authors Russell Archibald[1] and Harold Kerzner[2] documented this reality four decades ago and have continued to document it ever since. Whereas project managers tend to view project management quite personally, often with little or no distinction between their performance and the performance of the project, executives tend to view project management as a means to an end, as a good way of motivating people toward achievement of specific objectives, as a source of future executives, and as a means to achieve strategic objectives. On the negative side, project managers can see project management as a source of considerable frustration as they attempt to execute their responsibilities in the face of inadequate authority, misunderstanding, skepticism, and occasionally even hostile attitudes. Similarly negative, executives can see project management as an unsettling and possibly disruptive influence on the traditional organization, a necessary evil, a threat to their established authority, a cause for unwanted change to the status quo, and as unwanted evidence of deficiencies or failures in the traditional functional organization.

Figure 4.2 – Blind Men Parable

These differing viewpoints remind me of the blind men and the elephant parable as depicted in Figure 4.2. In that story, a group of blind men, who have never come across an elephant before, try to learn and conceptualize what the elephant is like by touching it. Each blind man feels a different part of the elephant body, but only one part, such as the side or the tusk. They then describe the elephant based on their partial experience and their descriptions are in complete disagreement on what an elephant is. In some versions, they come to suspect that the other person is dishonest, and they come to blows. The moral of the parable is that humans have a tendency to project their partial experiences, as the whole truth, ignore other people's partial experiences, and fail to consider that one may be partially right and may have partial information. What may appear to be common sense to one, may not to the other because, in my opinion, common sense requires common knowledge and/or experience.

I think that these differing viewpoints are driven, at least in part, by the fact that project work is quite different from the work in traditional functional organizations. The management concepts, policies, and attitudes that have been effective in those traditional organizations are not necessarily effective in project-driven organizations. Consequently, misunderstandings, friction, and downright resistance can develop not only from the project managers, but also from the executives. The executive environment comes complete with its own issues, barriers, and frustrations. A popular book about project sponsorship notes how some executives lament despite investing in raising the level of project manager competence, projects themselves still seem to take too long, cost too much, and produce fewer than the desired results.[3] For these executives, project management, in spite of how important it is to project managers, just does not seem but so important or so urgent; they have better things upon which to focus. Even the executive who is fully committed to acting for project success must confront the realities of executive and organizational life. The consequence of these realities is often a set of limitations or barriers challenging even the most motivated executive.

Project Management Knowledge Differs

Although project management may be second nature for project managers, that is unlikely to be the case for executives. A recent article in *CIO Magazine* by former Project Management Institute Chairman Antonio Nieto-Rodriguez suggests a couple of likely reasons.[4] He points out that in the *Harvard Business Review*, one of the gold standards for sources of business management thinking for almost one hundred years, fewer than one-half of one percent of the published articles have been about project management. Likewise for

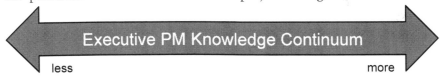

less   more

Figure 4.3 – Knowledge

business management education, only two of the top one hundred MBA programs in the world teach project management as a core course. Given this lack of attention in business publications and in business schools, it should come as no surprise that 80% of project management executives do not know how their projects align with their organization's business strategy,[5] or that one-third of all project failures are attributed to a lack of executive involvement.[6] It is no wonder that executives lack a basic understanding of project management, as illustrated in Figure 4.3, and are unsure how to act for project success.

I definitely do not advocate for executives to learn to be project managers. However, I do advocate for project managers to recognize this knowledge gap and to act accordingly. For example, this knowledge gap might be responsible for limiting the executive's appreciation or support for routinely spending significant time and effort on project planning and project requirements. That is because executives are more prone to seize business opportunities when they arise, for fear of losing them, with limited regard for the benefits of up front planning and requirements. The benefits of project planning and requirements can also be undercut by the impression, held by some executives, that those activities diminish the executive's authority. In those cases, the executive can feel threatened by the belief that the plans and requirements represent early decisions and commitments which constrain his or her reactionary, on-the-fly, and ad-hoc actions later. This level of accountability to planning and requirements can be seen as a threat to the executive's preference for flexibility.

Picking the right projects can be equally challenging. Opportunities that appear good for business may not necessarily appear to be as good for an available project manager. In these cases, the executive may consider project manager availability itself to be enough of a skill set, even when there is not a strong match in the experience and abilities needed for that particular project.

The impact of this knowledge gap between executives and project managers can be exacerbated by the common "hands off" style of some executives. For those executives, the pendulum to avoid micromanaging may have swung a bit too far in the other direction. The "I empower project managers to do anything they want as long as they meet milestones" type of approach may obfuscate important opportunities for the executive to take actions for project success. As pointed out by best-selling project management authors Harold Kerzner and Frank Saladis, a frequently missed action is to "create an environment where project management is viewed as a profession."[7]

Change Readiness Level

Executives and organizations are at varying levels of change readiness. It does little good to push for a change if the executive and/or the organization is not ready; in fact, it is counterproductive and "sours the well water" for future attempts at similar changes. High readiness levels are characterized by strong desires for change and readiness for it; a strong resistance to change characterizes low readiness levels. Moderate readiness levels are characterized by a desire for change but a lack of readiness. For example, if there was a merger yesterday, and if there is a reorganization today, then tomorrow would not be a good time for an executive to try to implement a substantial change to the organization's standard project life cycle. A more appropriate executive action would be to grant approval for a single project to tailor the standard life cycle in a way that benefits the project but does not broadly impact other projects and processes in the organization. The larger organization-wide change can wait. The executive actions must conform to the change readiness level of the organization as portrayed in Figure 4.4.

One of the factors which hinders change is the natural tendency for inertia. Just as in Newton's first law of motion, executives and organizations can be resistant to change because of how difficult or uncomfortable it can be. The notion of doing things this way because "this is the way we have always done them" can be particularly hard to overcome. To help address this problem, The Association of Change Management Professionals developed a *Standard for Change Management* that includes a process for assessing the organizational readiness for change.[8] This process assesses the preparedness of the conditions, attitudes, and resources needed for a change to happen successfully. It also focuses on assessing the level of comprehension, perceptions, and expectations of the change. The *Managing Change in Organizations Change Practice Guide* from PMI also includes useful information about assessing change readiness.[9] That document assesses change from the perspective of organizational systems, people, and culture.

Georgette was thrilled at the positive reaction she just received from the executive in her organization who had tasked her to study improving the organization's finance system. "Just what I was hoping for," he said. However, she was taken aback when he told her that he would not implement the improvements. He was moving on to a new assignment and would not be in a position to support implementing the improvements.

Figure 4.4 – Change Story

A number of models have been developed to help identify change readiness levels that are faithful to these change standards. A common example is ADKAR, an acronym that stands for awareness (of the business reasons for change), desire (to engage and participate in the change), knowledge (about how to change), ability (to realize or implement the change at the required performance level), and reinforcement (to ensure change sticks).[10] This model, as well as other effective models, provides objective insight into organization and individual readiness levels for changes, and highlights approaches for moving forward. A low readiness level in any of the areas can trigger a corresponding effort. If more awareness is needed, discuss and explore the reasons and benefits for this change. If more desire is needed, understand and address the inherent desire to change. If more knowledge is needed, focus on education and training for the skills and behaviors necessary to move forward. If more ability is needed, time may be necessary to develop new abilities and behaviors. If more reinforcement is needed, address the incentives or consequences for not continuing to act in the new way and revisit the knowledge and ability milestones.[11]

The barrier to executive actions for project success is at its lowest when there is an alignment between the type of action being considered and the change readiness level of the executive and the organization.

Organizational Maturity

Organizations are organic; they have attributes and may even be considered to have temperaments. Organizational behavior and social science come into play. Organizations impose limitations on what can be done by the executive. For example, it would do little good to push for an organization to adopt a standard project life cycle if that organization does not even practice project management. That approach would simply be too challenging a leap to make under those conditions. A more appropriate executive action would be to have a couple of appropriate activities managed as projects that use a life cycle approach; later on, after those first few projects have been successful, the executive could consider formalizing the life cycle process that was used. This "crawl before you walk" approach is reflected in the body of work that addresses organizational maturity.

Some of the notable early work in this area was performed at the Carnegie Mellon Software Engineering Institute with the development of a maturity model; that has since evolved into the Capability Maturity Model Integrated (CMMI).[12] This model can be used as a framework for appraising the process maturity of the organization. It can also be used to help integrate traditionally separate organizational functions, set process improvement goals and priorities, provide guidance for quality processes, and provide a point of reference for appraising current processes. The Organizational Project Management Maturity Model (OPM3) from PMI also includes useful information about assessing organizational maturity.[13] That document contains organizational maturity assessment processes that have been adapted for project, portfolio, and program management.

A useful attribute of these, as well as other, maturity models is the concept of levels. This attribute provides that each organization, or organizational element, exists at a specific and knowable level of maturity. The maturity level is established by assessing myriad characteristics of the organization;

weight is given for processes that are defined and repeatable. Once assessed, organizations can make defined changes, if they wish, to increase their maturity level. Another useful attribute of maturity models is the recognition that progression higher up the maturity scale must be done sequentially one level at a time, without skipping levels. Motivation for increasing an organization's maturity level is generally driven by a desire for the organization to be more effective and more efficient. Study findings in a recent *PMI Pulse of the Profession* report[14] indicate that projects are significantly more successful in higher maturity organizations.

These models show us that the lower maturity organizations are characterized by ad-hoc activity with little or no formal project procedures; individual heroics that occasionally result in success are rewarded. In contrast, formal, well-defined, and repeatable processes that are undergoing continuous improvement characterize high maturity organizations; success is intentional and can more easily be replicated.

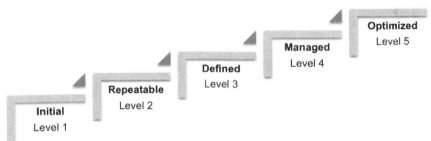

Figure 4.5 – Maturity Levels

A five-level maturity scale is illustrated in Figure 4.5. A level 1 organization has initial maturity: processes are typically undocumented and in a state of dynamic change and tend to be driven in an ad-hoc, uncontrolled, and reactive manner by users or events. A level 2 organization has repeatable maturity: some processes are repeatable, possibly with consistent results, process discipline is unlikely to be rigorous, but where it exists it may help to ensure that existing processes are maintained during times of stress.[15] Many, if not most, organizations or organizational elements that have conducted maturity assessments have been evaluated at level 2; I believe this is a factor that contributes to the preponderance of project managers who have expressed dissatisfaction with the level of executive support they have received. A level 3 organization has defined maturity: there are sets of defined and documented standard processes established and subject to some degree of improvement over time; these processes may not be systematically or repeatedly used to the degree necessary for the users to become competent or for the process to be validated in a range of situations. A level 4 organization has managed maturity: process metrics are used, effective achievement of the process objectives can be evidenced across a range of operational conditions, the suitability of the process in multiple environments has been tested and the process refined and adapted, and the process users have experienced the process in multiple and varied conditions and are able to demonstrate competence. A level 5 organization has optimized maturity: the focus is on continually improving process performance through both incremental and innovative changes.

I have conducted several organizational maturity assessments. In those instances, I found there was a desirable trade-off between simplicity and accuracy. In those circumstances, since rough approximations of the organizational maturity were adequate, relatively streamlined and imprecise assessments of the maturity of the organization were conducted. Those assessments provided enough insight into the aspects of the organizational elements that represented maturity limitations.

The barrier to executive actions for project success is at its lowest when there is an alignment between the type of action being considered and the maturity level of the organization. The executive actions must conform to the maturity level of the organization.

Organizational Politics

People, after all, are at the center of the executive's work life. And, in organizations where there are people, there is politics.[16] Organizational politics can subvert even a well-intentioned executive's action for project success in favor of the politically expedient. The field of project management, in particular, is fraught with politics, in large part because the ability to get things done is invariably shared among numerous entities. Additionally, the vast majority of projects exist outside of the traditional organizational structure, in a matrix configuration[17] where executives and project managers are relegated to the role of supernumerary. Neither the executive nor the project manager has sufficient levels of formal authority needed for project success. Add to this the cast of characters with roles as project stakeholders, and competing agendas invariably come into play. For example, it might be difficult for an executive in one organizational element to push for the entire organization to adopt the standard project life cycle used by that element if that version of the life cycle substantially conflicted with the version used in a different organizational element. A more appropriate action might be for the executives to partner rather than to compete.

Organizational politics are informal, unofficial, and sometimes behind-the-scenes efforts to sell ideas, influence an organization, increase power, or achieve other targeted objectives.[18] Politics has been around for millennia. Aristotle wrote that politics stems from a diversity of interests, and those competing interests must be resolved in some way. "Rational" alone may not work when interests are fundamentally incongruent, so political behaviors and influence tactics arise.

Organizational politics was at the top of the list of issues confronted by the executives I interviewed and surveyed.[19] That was expected; in a study reported in the *Academy of Management Journal*, 93% of executives surveyed reported that workplace politics exist in their organization, and 70% felt that in order to be successful, a person has to engage in politics.[20] It was identified as a leading source for conflicting demands on the executive, as the source for project scope creep, as a source of shifting of focus on project goals, and as a cause for fluctuations in staffing and financial resources. Short-term, bottom-line, mission-related demands were frequently cited as taking priority over longer-term strategic goals such as acting for project success. The "just get it done" mentality that can pervade other aspects of an organization can also dominate the executive's life. When executives were asked why they did not take more actions for project success, they invariably wove the topic of organizational politics into their answers.

The impact of organizational politics can extend beyond the executive also to affect the individual project team members. In an interesting review, individual project team members in organizations with high levels of organizational politics were found to show less interest in project-related outcomes and more interest in other activities with personal benefit.[21] These project team members were present physically but not mentally. Furthermore, when project team members perceived high levels of organizational politics and they still wanted to remain with their organization, they showed more political behavior to survive.

Organizational politics often come into play when dealing with the all-too-common issue of scarce resources. Executives and groups within the organization may disagree about how those resources should be allocated; therefore, they may naturally seek to gain those resources for themselves or for their interest groups, which gives rise to organizational politics. Executives may ally themselves with like-minded others in an attempt to win the scarce resources. They may engage in behavior such as bargaining, negotiating, alliance building, and resolving conflicting interests.

Numerous other factors can contribute to organizational politics. Executives who are highly self-motivated, who strive for excessive levels of control, or who have an elevated desire for power are prone to employ organizational politics. Organization pressure to succeed, to meet tight project deadlines, to compete, and to do more with less can also foster organizational politics. Organizational politics can thrive in cultures with low levels of trust, role and decision-making ambiguity, and unclear project and executive performance expectations.

Today, work in an organization requires skill in handling conflicting agendas and shifting power bases. Effective politics is not about winning at all costs but about maintaining relationships while achieving project results.[22] Although often portrayed negatively, organizational politics is not inherently bad. However, it is important to be aware of the potentially destructive aspects of organizational politics. Research reported in HR *Magazine* found that managers waste 20% of their time managing politics.[23]

The odds of an executive taking actions for project success are increased greatly when there is alignment between that action and the organizational politics at that point in time.

Limited Authority

As the project manager looks from his or her viewpoint, it might be easy to see the executive as someone with a sizeable amount of authority, especially relative to his or her own. Indeed, that may be the case in some situations. However, according to business guru and best-selling author Michael Porter, it is far more likely that the levels of executive authority fall short of what is needed for the executive to take actions for project success.[24] Even though the executive may bear full responsibility for the organization's well-being, he or she is apt to be a few steps removed from many of the factors needed to take those actions. Position and/or title alone does not confer the authority to lead, nor does it guarantee the loyalty of the organization. For example, it might be difficult for an executive to mandate the use of a standard project life cycle on projects in his or her element of the organization if a number of the project team members on those projects are matrixed from other elements in the organization that follow different life cycle methodologies. A more appropriate action might be to resolve the conflicts of authority for those project team members before addressing the subject of a standard project life cycle.

Although it seems to me that it is difficult for two writers to agree on a single, all-inclusive definition of "authority," I have come to appreciate it[25] "as the right to act or to direct the action of others in attainment of organizational goals." In the context of an organization engaged with projects, it can be seen as the power and right of an executive to use and allocate the resources efficiently, to make decisions and to give orders so as to achieve the project objectives. However, I think it important to recognize that in a typical matrix project environment, it is unlikely that the executive actually has direct authority over all of the elements and stakeholders necessary for project success. That authority is shared. Consequently, the successful completion of a project in terms of time, cost, and performance objectives is contingent upon the mutual understanding and acceptance of these authority patterns by all those with whom the executive must work.

Figure 4.6 – Matrix

One definition of a matrix organization that has stood the test of time is "any organization that employs a multiple command system that includes not only a multiple command structure but also related support mechanisms and an associated organizational culture and behavior pattern.[26] Note that the matrix structure violates the traditional management principles of unity of command and equality of authority with responsibility that were established many years ago by Henry Fayol.[27] It is this violation which makes delegation in matrix organizations infinitely more complex as represented in Figure 4.6. The interdisciplinary nature of projects in the multiple command structure of the matrix organization requires delegation by the executive to others in the organization not under his or her direct line supervision. Once authority is distributed or shared, the assignment of responsibility and the creation of accountability can become clouded. Responsibility refers to the assignment of duties that must be performed, milestones that must be reached, or tasks that must be completed in order to complete the project successfully. Accountability refers to the obligation to perform the assigned work.

This limitation of executive authority is at the root of a common quandary for executives, a quandary that occurs with a key executive function: resources. The wheels of project progress grind to a halt fairly quickly when resources dry up. People and money are needed in amounts and on the timeline specified in the project plan. Unfortunately, executives are hampered in their ability to supply these resources. According to a study published in the *Harvard Business Review*, only 42% of executives have direct responsibility for their budgets.[28] The majority of the study respondents reported that they were at the mercy, at least in part, of others to supply project resources. And, when resources are supplied, only 30% of the executives thought that the resources were sufficient for project success.[29]

In what some may consider a perverse twist in organizations where "money talks," limited authority and resources create a self-reinforcing cycle. Limited authority contributes to limited resources which contributes to limited authority.

The odds of an executive taking actions for project success are increased greatly when there is alignment between the level of authority needed for that action to succeed and the level of authority of the executive.

Measurement Model

Models to measure various aspects of management, leadership, organizational, and individual behavior have repeatedly proven their worth. Typically, these models present a simplified view of what is depicted graphically in two dimensions, the model's characteristics are explained, and information is given for how the model can be used to guide action.[30]

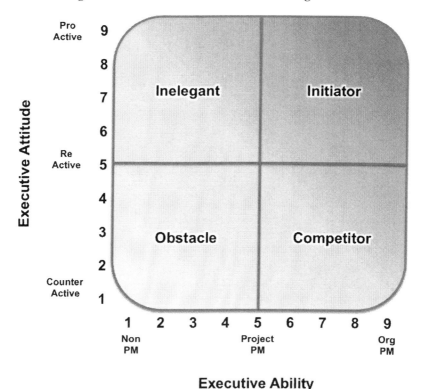

Figure 4.7 – Executive Support For Projects Model

As useful as these existing models may be, I have not found them especially relevant for the task of assessing levels of executive support for projects and the corresponding barriers to executive action. Consequently, I developed a new model specifically for this purpose. This new model, shown in Figure 4.7, includes scales for assessing the attitude and ability of the executive toward taking actions for project success. I developed this *Executive Support for Projects* model as an aid in assessing and in diagnosing the organizational environment in which the project manager and executive reside. Armed with a level of understanding about the nature of an executive's support for projects, the project manager is more likely to be able to find an effective approach to help the executive take the actions for project success. Note that the model represents the observable behavior of the executive and can be used to assist with determining the underlying reasons for this behavior.

The Executive Attitude axis is presented as a continuum that represents the attitude of the executive toward taking actions for project success. At the high end of the scale, executives are characterized as proactive: taking initiative to identify and act on opportunities that they see as supportive of project success. The midpoint on the scale pertains to executives who are reactive, those who take supportive action in response to a stimulus from the situation or project manager. The low end of the scale represents behavior that is counter to the goal of acting for project success; actions taken at this end of the scale reduce the likelihood of project success.

The Executive Ability axis is offered as a continuous range representing the ability of the executive to overcome barriers to taking action. At the high end of the scale, executives are characterized as being adept at not only the management of a project-based organization, but also in the management of the projects; organizational change is a skill possessed by these executives. The midpoint on the scale pertains to executives who have a full set of skills to manage within the bounds of a defined project, but who are not equipped to impact the organizational environment in which the project is located. The low end of the scale represents executives who, although they may possess a significant range of skills, are not able to manage within the project environment.

By using the *Executive Support For Projects* model, the project manager can gauge both the executive's attitude and ability; an example of the application of this model is illustrated in Figure 4.8. Taken together, these two dimensions can serve as the basis of understanding needed to allow the project manager to help the executive overcome the barriers and accelerate support for project success. The resulting *Executive Support For Projects* behavior quadrants are as follows:

Initiator Behavior: Proactive attitude and organizational project management ability. Concern for taking actions for project success. Thorough knowledge of the management of projects within the organizational context. High motivation to use foresight to identify upcoming opportunities. Project manager can benefit by using full and open communications with the executive to ensure that actions for project success are synchronized.

Inelegant Behavior: Proactive attitude and non-project management ability. Concern for taking action for project success, but without the benefit of needed understanding about project management. Likelihood of well-intentioned actions being taken that are less than effective. Project manager can benefit from taking the lead to identify the actions for the executive to take and by helping the executive take these actions.

Competitor Behavior: Counteractive attitude and organizational project management ability. Concern for agendas counter to project success. Thorough knowledge of the management of projects within the organizational context. Likelihood of subjugating project management to achieve competing agenda. Project manager can benefit from keeping well informed of the executive actions and by looking for common ground to reduce the level of competition.

Obstacle Behavior: Counteractive attitude and non-project management ability. Concern for agendas counter to project success but without the benefit of needed understanding about project management. Likelihood of somewhat random and unpredictable behavior that

George wants to get his executive to act for project success and has decided that his executive falls within the Obstacle quadrant as someone who knows little about project management and whose actions are counter to George's goal of boosting authority with a project charter. George begins working with his executive to educate him about some project management basics so that his executive can appreciate the need George has to demonstrate authority. Over time, as the executive's appreciation about project management increases, so does his interest and ability to support George. Over time, the behavior of George's executive moves more toward the center of the Executive Ability and Executive Support quadrant.

Figure 4.8 – Model Story

may or may not impact project success. Project manager can benefit from some insulation from and resilience to the executive, from an alliance with a more supportive executive, and from efforts to raise the project management knowledge level of the executive.

Chapter Highlights

Executives, even when they are knowledgeable about actions necessary for project success and when they are motivated to take those actions, face barriers. It is essential for project managers who want to help get their executives to act for project success to understand these executive barriers. To aid project managers in assessing and diagnosing the organizational environment in which the project manager and executive reside, I have developed a new *Executive Support for Projects* model. Common executive barriers listed in this book include the following:

- Viewpoints differ
- Project management knowledge differs
- Change readiness level
- Organizational maturity
- Organizational politics
- Limited authority

---

[1] Archibald, R. (1976). *Managing high-technology programs & projects*. New York, NY: John Wiley & Sons. This first edition of this book, as well as the subsequent second and third editions, included an insightful treatment of the differing views of project management.

[2] Kerzner, H. (1979). *Project management: A systems approach to planning, scheduling, and controlling*. New York, NY: John Wiley & Sons. The first edition of this book, as well as all subsequent editions, included an insightful treatment of the differing views of project management. This book, which has now been published in its 12th edition, is considered by many to be "the bible" of project management.

[3] Englund, R., & Bucero, A. (2015). *Project sponsorship (second edition)*. San Francisco, CA: Jossey-Bass. The authors advocated for a formally established project sponsor role and advocate for executive-level individuals to fulfill that role.

[4] Nieto-Rodriguez, B. (2016). Why senior executives neglect project management. *CIO Magazine.* Retrieved January 22, 2018, from https://www.cio.com/article/3144510/project-management/why-senior-executives-neglect-project-management.html. This article made the point that executives do not recognize the value of project management and that the lack of awareness can lead to problems with strategy execution.

[5] Changepoint. (2017). Turning around a failing pmo. *Changepoint.* Retrieved January 22, 2018, from https://www.changepoint.com/blog/turning-around-failing-pmo. This article linked the high failure rate of PMOs to lack of executive support.

[6] Emam, K., & Koru, A. (2008). A replicated survey of IP software project failures. *IEEE Software Journal 0740-7459/08.* Washington, DC. IEEE Computer Society. The multi-year study findings identified leading causes of project failures.

[7] Kerzner, H., & Saladis, F. (2009). *What executives need to know about project management.* Hoboken, NJ: John Wiley & Sons. The authors included details about basic project management principles and then addressed how executives could serve as project sponsors.

[8] Association of Change Management Professionals. (2014). *Standard for Change Management.* Winter Springs, FL: Association of Change Management Professionals. This standard described the areas of knowledge, established norms, processes, tasks, ands skills necessary for change management practitioners to be effective in managing change in their industries and organizations; it is complementary to project management.

[9] Project Management Institute. (2013). *Managing change in organizations: a practice guide.* Newtown Square, PA: Project Management Institute. This document set the practices, processes, and disciplines on managing change in the context of portfolio, program, and project management and illustrated how change management has been an essential ingredient in using project management as the vehicle for delivering organizational strategy.

[10] Prosci. (2006). *ADKAR: a model for change in business, government and our community.* Fort Collins, CO: Prosci Learning Center Publications. When applied to organizational change, this model allowed leaders and change management teams to focus their activities on what will drive individual change and, therefore, achieve organizational results.

[11] Kotter, J. (2012). *Leading change.* Brighton, MA: Harvard Business Review Press. I have found the subject of organizational change to be well represented in the business literature. John Kotter's now-legendary eight-step process for managing change with positive results has become the foundation for leaders and organizations across the globe.

[12] CMMI Institute. (2010). *CMMI for development (version 1.3).* Pittsburg, PA: Software Engineering Institute. The CMMI Institute was acquired by the Information Systems Audit and Control Association.

[13] Project Management Institute. (2013). *Organizational project management maturity model (third edition).* Newtown Square, PA: Project Management Institute. This document provided processes to assess an organization's practices against best practices. The assessment findings, without being prescriptive, could be used to guide an organization to undertake relevant changes.

[14] Project Management Institute. (2016). *Pulse of the profession: the high cost of low performance.* Newtown Square, PA: Project Management Institute. This global survey publication findings showed that 71% of projects succeed in organizations with high project management maturity vs. 52% success in low maturity organizations.

[15] Although accurate reporting of assessed organizational maturity levels is scarce, it appears to me that the unofficial average level is no higher than a two (on a five-point scale) for organizations in the U.S. The average level of the officially published appraisal results from the CMMI Institute is about three.

[16] Pinto, J. (1996). *Power & politics in project management.* Newtown Square, PA: Project Management Institute. This book offered an early and comprehensive look into the role organizational politics plays in project implementation. The author was the lead faculty member for Penn State's Master of Project Management program and the author or editor of 23 books and over 120 scientific papers that have appeared in a variety of academic and practitioner journals, books, conference proceedings, and technical reports.

[17] Organizations can be characterized as functional, matrix, or projectized. In a functional organization, there is a hierarchy where each employee has one clear senior, and staff members are grouped by specialty. In a projectized organization, the project manager serves as the one clear senior for all team members, regardless of specialty. Matrix organizations reflect a blend of functional and projectized where staff report to both a project manager and a functional manager.

[18] Brandon, R., & Seldman, M. (2004). *Survival of the savvy: high-integrity political tactics for career and company success.* New York, NY: Free Press. Note that there is a lack of consensus among authors for the definition of the term "organizational politics."

[19] O'Brochta, M. (2006, February-May). *Interviews With CIA Project Management Executives*, Washington D.C.: Unpublished interviews with two dozen executives working in a project-based element of the organization.

[20] Gandz, J., & Murray, V. (1980). The experience of workplace politics. *Academy of Management Journal, 23*, 237–251. This study investigated the perceived politicization of organizational processes and their attitudes and beliefs about workplace politics.

[21] Saeed, M., Butt, A., & Azam, N. (2013). *Effects of organizational politics, organizational commitment, organizational communication, and task delegation on the individual project team member's performance.* International Conference on Safety, Construction Engineering and Project Management Proceedings 2013. Islamabad, Pakistan. The study findings suggested that executives should focus their organizational politics strategies in such a way that their project team members remain committed to project goals.

[22] I advocate for the adoption of the positive perspective of organizational politics, where the project, and not a personal agenda, is the central focus of the politics.

[23] Valle, M., & Perrewe, P. (2000). Do politics perceptions relate to political behaviors? Tests of an implicit assumption and expanded model. *Human Relations, 53*, 359–386. This study examined perceived political behaviors as a critical, yet largely overlooked, component in the traditional organizational politics perceptions model.

[24] Porter, M., Lorsch, J., & Nohria, N. "Seven Surprises for New CEOs." R0410C. *Harvard Business Review* 82, no. 10 (October 2004): 62–72. Michael Porter has been an economist, researcher, author, advisor, speaker, and teacher. Throughout his career at Harvard Business School, he has brought economic theory and strategy concepts to bear on many of the most challenging problems facing corporations, economies, and societies. His extensive research has received numerous awards, and he has been the most-cited scholar today in economics and business.

[25] Sisk, H. (1999). *Management and organization (international second edition).* Cincinnati, OH: Thompson South-Western Publishing Company. Numerous editions of this book have been used in foundational courses in colleges and universities.

[26] Davis, S., & Lawrence, P. (1977). *Matrix.* Reading, Massachusetts: Addison-Wesley Publishing Company. More recently, PMI included a projectized version of this definition in the PMBOK Guide as "any organizational structure in which the project manager shares responsibility with the functional managers for assigning priorities and for directing the work of persons assigned to the project."

[27] Henri Fayol (1841-1925), who is considered by many as the founder for today's modern scientific management, developed 14 principles of management.

[28] Prahalad, C., & Hamel, G. (1990). The core competence of the corporation. *Harvard Business Review*. Retrieved January 22, 2018, from https://hbr.org/1990/05/the-core-competence-of-the-corporation. Prahalad has been described by HBR as one of the world's "wisest and most influential management thinkers." This document urged leaders to rethink the concept of the corporation itself, from a portfolio of businesses managed and optimized independently, to a portfolio of competencies spanning across individual businesses and delivering real and sustaining competitive advantage.

[29] Buchanan, D., Denyer, D., & Jaina, J. "How do they manage, a qualitative study of the realities of middle and front-line management." *Health Services and Delivery Research*, No. 1.4 (June 2013). This extensive study gathered data from 1,200 managers.

[30] I have come to rely on the Managerial Grid Model introduced by Blake in 1964 for insights regarding concern for people versus concern for production, the Transactional/Transformational Leadership Model introduced by Burns in 1978 for insights regarding working within the organizational culture versus changing the organizational culture, and the Strength Deployment Inventory Model introduced by Porter in 1971 for insight into leadership motivation and related behavior.

Chapter 5

TAKE PROJECT MANAGER STEPS

"It's not what we know but how we use what we know that counts."
James Elliott 1882-1946
Marketing executive

Getting To The Goal

The goal is for executives to act for project success. Getting to that goal involves you, the project manager, taking steps to help your executive overcome the barriers to taking those actions. This involves taking initiative and challenging the status quo. This challenging the status quo entails building upon and reinforcing a strong mutual partnership between project managers and executives. When successful, this becomes a "let me help you to help me" type of situation where you take the steps to help the executive overcome the barriers, who, in turn, then takes actions for project success; see Figure 5.1 for a list of steps a project managers can take.

Speak Truth To Power

The commonly acknowledged flashpoint for the spread of the phrase "speak truth to power" was a 1995 publication that popularized what was an obscure Quaker saying from a century and a half ago.[1] In the context of this book, "speaking" refers to the project manager having a say, "truth" refers to the list of executive actions, and "power" refers to the executive. In other words, the project manager speaks to the more powerful executive in a way that motivates the executive to accept help from the project manager and then to take actions for project success.

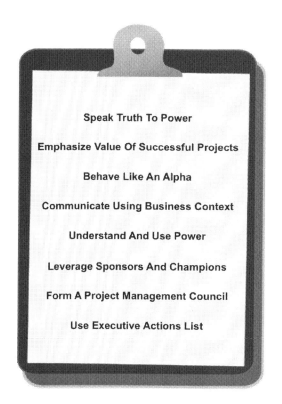

Speak Truth To Power

Emphasize Value Of Successful Projects

Behave Like An Alpha

Communicate Using Business Context

Understand And Use Power

Leverage Sponsors And Champions

Form A Project Management Council

Use Executive Actions List

Figure 5.1 – Project Manager Steps

Speaking truth to power may summon a bit of fear: of being noticed, of being attacked, or of being punished. It may arouse some self-limiting concerns that "it is not my place," or "I won't be listened to," or "the executive should already know." After all, recent research reported in the *Harvard Business Review* reveals that executives simply do not appreciate how risky it can feel for others to speak up.[2] Fortunately, there are a couple of approaches when speaking truth to power that can offset these fears and self-limiting concerns.[3] The speaking must be wholly truthful, devoid of self-interest, without harming any innocents, and without spite or anger; authenticity is key. Equally fortunate, these approaches have been developed into a five-step plan that can be used by project managers looking to strengthen their ability to communicate with executives.[4] First, and foremost, know your facts, state your case, stand your ground, keep your cool, and offer options. One of the most effective options is for you, the project manager, to offer to help.

Influencing without authority comes into play when speaking truth to power. Fortunately, this subject has benefited from some insightful work reflected in a number of notable books,[5] including the now classic *Influence Without Authority*. That treatment of the subject centers on the concept of an influence model where you trade what they want in exchange for what you have, a type of negotiation. The model begins with the assumption that all are potential allies, then moves on to the stage where you clarify your goals and priorities, you diagnose the world of the other person, you identify relevant currencies for both yourself and the other person involved, you identify the nature of the relationship between you and the other person, and you select a trading approach and make exchanges. When successful, you will be in a better position to speak about the executive actions for project success.

Emphasize Value Of Successful Projects

When executives are focused on the organizational bottom line, then you, the project manager, can get their attention by emphasizing the contribution successful projects and mature project management practices make to that bottom line. Study findings in a recent PMI *Pulse of the Profession* report[6] showed that projects within organizations that adhere to proven project management practices meet original goals and business intent 90% of the time versus only 36% of the time for organizations not adhering to proven project management practices. Those organizations using proven project management practices wasted about 13 times less money than the low performers. The report points out that one of the significant contributors to the remarkably better performance of the organizations using proven project management practices is the attention they pay to aligning their projects to the organizational strategy and goals.

Project management is key to getting new corporate initiatives accomplished. For the past two decades, the standard of excellence for research in the new product development area has been set through the examination by Dr. Robert Cooper of more than 2,000 new product launches at hundreds of companies.[7] This research has clearly identified that the theme is the need for speed and its companion need for change. The research shows that nothing is static, markets are fluid, and needs change at a far faster rate today than ever before. This demand for speed, coupled with fluid markets, requires reducing the cycle time between concept and product. Project management is about the management of cycle time; it is about tailoring the variety of available life cycles to the particulars of a given project to increase the probability of success. As such, project management serves as a critical enabler for executive success in the environment that rewards speed.

When executives are focused on their own bottom line, then you can get their attention by emphasizing the contribution that successful projects and mature project management practices make to their own careers. Successful projects are critically important to the executive who understands that the number one reason for executive failure is not lack of vision or strategy. According to a cover story in *Fortune Magazine*,[8] "It's bad execution. As simple as that: not getting things done, being indecisive, not delivering on commitments." Furthermore, "while average CEO tenure in the biggest companies has remained fairly steady at seven to eight years, those who do not deliver are getting pushed out quicker…poorly performing CEOs are three times more likely to get booted than they were a generation ago. Either they deliver, soon, or they're gone."

Additionally, since project management is all about getting things done and delivering on commitments, it is very well positioned to be the cornerstone upon which executive success is built. Projects by definition involve delivering a product or service at a defined point in time, just what the executive needs to achieve success in his or her jobs. The way I see it, the executive's career is actually dependent on project success. You can raise awareness of this dependency as a key toward gaining executive interest and support for taking actions for project success. It is, after all, in the executive's self-interest.

Behave Like An Alpha

Since executives benefit from successful projects, they are well served by relying on the top project managers for those successes. Project managers find many benefits from performing at the top level as well.

Figure 5.2 – Alphas

A survey of over 5,000 project managers, stakeholders, and executives has provided an extraordinary insight into what the top two percent of project managers know and do that everyone else does not.[9] This is one of my favorite studies of all time because it gets to the heart of successful project management. This study focused on identifying the best project managers, referred to as Alpha project managers, and then on determining what they did that made them the best. Opinions about these project managers were obtained from team members, customers, and management. Opinions were focused on eight specific areas: attitude and belief, communication, approach and alignment, organization, focus and prioritization, issue management, relationships and conflict, and leadership. As illustrated in Figure 5.2, the study results revealed large differences between what the Alpha project managers believe and do versus the non-Alpha project managers.

The Alphas were found to believe strongly that they had enough authority to manage the project, 89 percent for Alphas vs. 49 percent for non-Alphas. This data supports the maxim for project managers to "take action and ask forgiveness later." Alphas, who had the attitude they were empowered and behaved accordingly, had a greater level of authority conferred upon them.

The Alphas also distinguished themselves when planning projects. Although the study revealed both Alphas and non-Alphas understood equally the importance of planning, the Alphas dedicated double the amount of project time to do the actual planning. Alphas spent on average a total of 21% of all project labor hours on planning. This additional planning time became available as a result of the keen focus Alphas had on prioritization. Alphas responded to fewer emails per day, spent less time in meetings, and were effective at prioritizing the myriad demands on their time.

And, the Alphas also distinguished themselves when communicating. Both Alphas and non-Alphas equally understood the value of communication; however, the Alphas were viewed by others as being much more effective at performing the actual communication, 80% for Alphas vs. 49% for non-Alphas. The communication they paid the most attention to was with their stakeholders; Alphas constantly asked others for their opinions about the project, and they responded with information tailored to their stakeholder interests.

Armed with this survey information, you now understand that you can enjoy the benefits of being an Alpha if you assume more authority, increase the amount of planning you do, and increase the effectiveness of your communication. As an Alpha, you are more likely to get your executive to act for project success.

Communicate Using Business Context

How you communicate with your executive has at least as much effect as what you communicate. Even a well-crafted project management message will fall flat if the executive fails to hear it. Consequently, learning how to frame your message can be a big asset as illustrated in Figure 5.3.

Much has been done to elevate the level of understanding of how to communicate project management to executives.[10] The findings from a research study involving two thousand project personnel, consultants,

Georgette was shocked when her request for additional project funding was turned down by her executive. She thought her statements about using the additional funding to increase the transmitter antenna gain by 6dB were crystal clear. Thankfully, her request was approved when she returned some time later to explain that the additional funding would double the transmitter range and half the requirements to staff the system.

Figure 5.3 – Context Story

and executives reveal that effective communication between project manager and executive begins long before the message is passed; it begins by building a relationship first. Once that is achieved, this excellent body of work instructs project managers to emphasize alignment of project management and project goals with corporate goals and value statements. It identifies the value of using business language and putting the project in context of business value where project aspects that relate to financial, growth, customer satisfaction, competition, and sales are emphasized.

A key that appears throughout the topic of communicating with executives about project management is the need for you to identify what specifically triggers the executive's interest, to develop a set of responses tailored to each trigger, and to back up each response with evidence that is relevant to each individual executive. If the executive's hot button is growth, then you are well-served to frame the project management-related action for the executive in terms of growth. Interestingly, the study identified one particular hot button as being particularly effective: a crises. Specifically, a crises pressured executives to consider the merits of project management in terms of the business problem. They became open to the idea that improving project management processes was a type of insurance policy against future outbreaks of a similar crises.

You can build a relationship with your executive so that when the time comes, you can couch the project management actions you want him or her to take in the business context that resonates most.

Understand And Use Power

As a project manager, you have at your disposal an extremely effective tool for overcoming barriers and getting your executive to act for project success: power. Admittedly, most project managers I have encountered react to this statement with a bit of surprise, a bit of skepticism, and a bit of curiosity. They seem to have concluded previously that in their roles as project managers they were practically powerless. I have heard project managers lament on many occasions that it seemed practically everyone else in their organization had more power than they did. However, once they have been introduced to the subject of power, their skepticism begins to melt away, and their curiosity surges. This is a favorite subject of mine.

Through the understanding and use of power, you can accomplish a tremendous amount. Power refers to the ability of the project manager to influence others to act for the benefit of his or her project; it is a resource that enables compliance or commitment from others.[11] In what has become a widely accepted classification of power, John French and Bertram Raven, identified five bases of power as shown in Figure 5.4: coercive, expert, legitimate, referent, and reward.[12] Their work continues to be the cornerstone against which other treatments of the subject of power are centered.

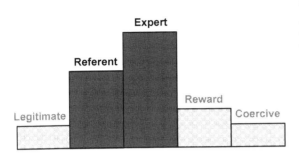

Figure 5.4 – Bases Of Power

Unsurprisingly, you as a project manager have little of what is commonly referred to as legitimate power; this comes from a formally appointed position or title. For similar reasons, you likely have little coercive or reward power; without control over salaries or promotions, there is not much a project manager can take away from or give to a co-worker or executive. However, you do have, and you can further develop, expert and referent power.

Expert power is based on your knowledge, experience, and special skills. When you recognize that you are indeed an expert, you can begin to use your power. Your expertise is centered around what you know about your project. It is possible, even likely, that no one else in the world knows as much about your project, or your portion of the project, as you do. This makes you the expert. When you exercise your expert power properly, others will come to rely on your knowledge and to trust you as a dependable information source.

Referent power is based on the affiliations you have with other groups and individuals; the larger your network of affiliations and the more people in your network with power, the more referent power you have. Fortunately, as a project manager who is likely working in a matrix organization, you have been placed in an excellent position to develop a sizeable network. A matrix organizational structure, by its very definition, brings you in contact with multiple reporting chains, multiple bosses, and multiple departments. When you develop your network of affiliations, others will come to rely on you for who you know and for who knows you.

An illustration of expert power and to some degree referent power can be found in one of the highest-rated television shows in history, MASH. This show, which was broadcast from 1972-1983 and has been in continual reruns ever since, revolved around a Mobile Army Surgical Unit in the Korean War. As the show developed, the viewers were introduced to a number of characters, including a Colonel, a Major, a Captain, several doctors, and a clerk. One of the characters emerged as the most powerful, the clerk named Radar. Others, regardless of rank, looked to him because of what and who he knew. He had a savant-like ability to know things before they happened.

John Kotter, New York Times best-selling author and Harvard professor, regarded as an authority on leadership, made significant contributions to the subject of power and influence.[13] He has addressed how to get things done through others by building a power base when your responsibilities exceed your formal authority. That power base can be built by forming strong lateral relationships, by building a track record and reputation, and by developing expert knowledge. Other authors refer to this as soft power, the ability to attract and co-opt.[14]

I want to draw your attention to an aspect of your behavior that can enable you to continue to grow your power or short circuit your power altogether: ethics. As the former Chair of the PMI Ethics Member Advisory Group, I developed a keen awareness of the role ethics plays in your power.[15] My belief is that project manager power, like the kind called for in this book, is only effective if there are people who respond to that power. For that to happen, there must be trust based on ethical behavior. In *The Leadership Challenge*, which continues to be a best seller after six editions and 20 years in print[16] and which is considered the gold standard for research-based leadership, the text informs us that leadership requires trust: "It's clear that if people anywhere are to willingly follow someone, whether it be into battle or into the boardroom, the front office or the front lines, they first want to assure themselves that the person is worthy of their trust." One of the most effective ways to build trust is to abide by the four values in the PMI Code of Ethics and Professional Conduct: responsibility, respect, honesty, and fairness.[17] Transgressions in any one of these four values can cause immediate and long-lasting undercutting of trust.

As you make conscious efforts to develop and grow your expert and referent power, be aware that power has no steady state. You are either gaining or loosing power; it does not remain constant. So, if power is a subject that you have not given much attention to, you likely have low levels of it. Likewise, if power is a subject that you are not currently putting much effort into, then you are likely losing what little power you had. For this reason, I advocate for project managers to look consciously and continuously for opportunities to grow their power. One of the most effective ways for you to do that is through effective communication. Tailoring specific information about something you are expert in, such as your project, and delivering that tailored information to a key stakeholder at a point in time that is important for them will grow your power. The timing of this communication is important. In recognition of the power of short-term self-interest, leading research-based project management author Jeffrey Pinto, in a first-of-its-kind book[18] on the subject of power and politics in project management, observes that "one of the hardest lessons for newcomers to organizations to learn is the consistently expressed and displayed primacy of departmental loyalties and self-interest over organization-wide concerns." Repeating that communication focused on the short-term self-interest of other key stakeholders at other points in time will further grow your power. With sufficient levels of power, you will be much more likely to get your executive to act for project success.

Leverage Sponsors And Champions

You can build your power by developing and harnessing the power of project sponsors and champions. Project sponsors are recognized as persons or groups who provide support for the project and are key to raising project success rates. When PricewaterhouseCoopers conducted their 2012 global survey on the state of project management,[19] they found that "lack of executive sponsorship was the second largest factor that contributed to poor project performance." Since project sponsors have considerably more power than you, the project manager, they can effectively boost what power you do have. Sponsor duties include seller, coach and mentor, filter, business judge, motivator, negotiator, protector, and most importantly, supporter.[20] Effective project sponsors are decision makers, they are influential, they remove project road blocks, and they act quickly to resolve project issues.

For those project managers unable to round up all of the necessary sponsor support, an alternative has emerged, the project champion. This role is increasing in importance given that, according to a recent *PMI Pulse of the Profession* report, sponsors are frequently in short supply and overextended.[21] In this informal role, there exists a key lieutenant of the sponsor who is likely more approachable and accessible then the sponsor.[22] Here, we have an individual with authority who is trusted by the sponsor and who can work directly with the project manager. Here, we have a connection path for the project manager to sources of higher authority in the organization. The project champion can advocate for and support the project, represent the project and project manager to executives, and run interference for the project manager.

Building your power through effective project sponsor and champion relationships can help you reach the point where your executive will be inclined to act for project success.

Form A Project Management Council

And now for an approach that can work in countless situations, with differing viewpoints, with differing levels of project management knowledge, across change readiness levels, and in the midst of organizational politics. The approach is for you to form a project management council. It can be a key to identifying the actions for the executive to take for project success, and it can amplify your power to get executives to act for project success. If one project management voice is good, two voices are better, and a group of voices is even better.

This is a favorite approach of mine. I have used it often, and so have many others.[23] Referred to variously as a project support office, project management working group, project management office, strategic project office, project management center of excellence, and project management community of practice, these are organizations formed explicitly for the purpose of focusing on how project management is, can, and should be practiced within the organization. I am using the term "Project Management Council" to include these and any other mechanisms that bring together, formally or informally, like-minded project management voices.

My ideal project management council is comprised entirely of motivated project management practitioners who have volunteered for the assignment. They are experienced, visionary change agents. As thought leaders, they know how project management is done and how it should be done. They care deeply about their chosen profession, are concerned with the well-being of other project managers, and care about the success of their organization.

A project management council can and should serve as a link between project managers and executives. Sizing it to no more than about a dozen people, having it chaired and/or sanctioned by an executive, and limiting its authority will help it gain recognition for the good it can do and help it counter many of the stereotypical negatives associated with groups of this type that exist outside the formal organization chart. Having it focus broadly on the entire organizational system as it relates to projects and project management raises its bona fides. Having it make recommendations to executives and provide help with implementing the executive actions positions it to have enduring value. Precluding it from control over decisions and resources minimizes the possibility that it will be viewed as a threat to established organizational decision-making mechanisms. Limiting the term of its members to a year or possibly two will ensure a constant flow of fresh perspectives and ideas. Chartering the project management council to identify the barriers to project success and to make recommendations to overcome these barriers and then giving it the latitude to explore the paths that follow will invigorate its members as well as the organization.

You can greatly amplify your voice by assembling a group of like-minded project managers to tailor the list of executive actions, to strengthen your message, and to offer to assist the executive in carrying out actions for project success.

Use Executive Actions List

A number of experienced project managers and authors have been articulate about the actions that they would like their executives to take. I have listed and elaborated on those actions in this book; see Figure 5.5. You can, and should, build upon the solid basis for the list in this book by blending your experience and your judgment, by reflecting upon the unique circumstances of your project and your organization, and by soliciting inputs from your fellow project managers. Then, make your own tailored executive actions list. Tailor your executive actions list with the reality of what can be achieved in your specific situation at a specific point in time.

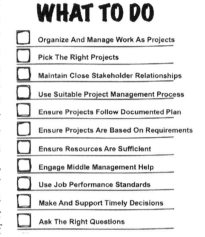

WHAT TO DO

☐ Organize And Manage Work As Projects

☐ Pick The Right Projects

☐ Maintain Close Stakeholder Relationships

☐ Use Suitable Project Management Process

☐ Ensure Projects Follow Documented Plan

☐ Ensure Projects Are Based On Requirements

☐ Ensure Resources Are Sufficient

☐ Engage Middle Management Help

☐ Use Job Performance Standards

☐ Make And Support Timely Decisions

☐ Ask The Right Questions

Figure 5.5 – List

That tailoring should take into account barriers to executive action, including the reality that your executive has a different viewpoint and level of project management knowledge than you do. It should also reflect the change readiness level of the executive and the organization, the organizational maturity, the state of the organizational politics, and the limited authority of the executive.

With the tailored list in hand, it is time to plan. Getting executives to act for project success is, after all, a project. As such, planning is in order. This planning need not be complex or lengthy, but it certainly needs to include a time-based sequence of the tasks and clear criteria to measure project success. I have found it beneficial to configure those tasks to focus on one or two of the executive actions first and to avoid trying to do too much at once. Incremental progress is best, one step at a time. Iterative progress is important too, by incorporating the feedback and lessons learned from the implementation on the first couple of executive actions.

With the plan in hand, you will be ready to speak truth to power. When you behave like an Alpha and communicate using business context, you will begin to build your power. Your power will grow after you understand and begin using it. Your power will continue to grow as you leverage champions and sponsors and as you form a project management council. Along the way, you will be successful getting your executive to take actions for project success.

Chapter Highlights

The goal is for executives to act for project success. Getting to that goal involves you, the project manager, taking steps to help your executive overcome the barriers to taking those actions. This process involves building upon and reinforcing a strong mutual partnership between you and your executive to challenge the status quo. It involves establishing and building your power base. Project manager steps identified in this book include the following:

- Speak truth to power
- Emphasize value of successful projects
- Behave like an Alpha
- Communicate using business context
- Understand and use power
- Leverage sponsors and champions
- Form a project management council
- Use executive actions list

Chapter End Notes

[1] American Friends Service Committee. (1955). *Speak truth to power: a quaker search for an alternative to violence*. Philadelphia, PA: American Friends Service Committee. This book explored the politics of non-violence. Its title has since been adopted as a phrase in the business world to refer to situations in which an individual with limited power interacts with someone who has higher levels of power.

[2] Reitz, M., & Higgins, J. (2017, March). The problem with saying "my door is always open." *Harvard Business Review*. Retrieved January 22, 2018, from https://hbr.org/2017/03/the-problem-with-saying-my-door-is-always-open#comment-section. Findings from a two-year research study provided insight into aspects of openness overlooked by executives.

[3] O'Toole, J. (2015, October). Speaking truth to power: a white paper. *Markkula Center for Applied Ethics*. Retrieved January 22, 2018, from https://www.scu.edu/ethics/focus-areas/business-ethics/resources/speaking-truth-to-power-a-white-paper. This white paper included the powerful quote from Herbert Agar's book *A Time for Greatness*: "The truth that makes men free is for the most part the truth which men prefer not to hear."

[4] Eblin, S. (2011, September). A five-step plan for speaking truth to power. *Business Management Daily*. Retrieved January 22, 2018, from https://www.businessmanagementdaily.com/20963/a-five-step-plan-for-speaking-truth-to-power. This article captured the important steps taken by former Congressional Budget Office Director Doug Elmendorf when he was the star witness at a hostile Congressional committee hearing.

[5] Cohen, A, & Bradford, D. (2017). *Influence without authority (third edition)*. Hoboken, NJ: John Wiley & Sons. This book takes the position that nobody has enough formal authority to achieve what is necessary. Other books on this subject worth considering include the following: *Influencer* by Joseph Grenny, *Crucial Conversations* by Kerry Patterson, and *Getting to Yes* by Roger Fisher.

[6] Project Management Institute. (2015). *Pulse of the profession: capturing the value of project management*. Newtown Square, PA: Project Management Institute. This global survey publication findings continued to reinforce that when organizations embrace repeatable project, program, and portfolio management practices, they have better outcomes.

[7] Cooper, R. (2017). *Winning at new products: creating value through innovation*. New York, NY: Basic Books. This is a fully updated edition of the classic research-driven business reference book on product development.

[8] Charan, R., & Colvin, G. (1999, June). Why ceos fail. *Fortune Magazine*. This milestone article spawned a number of follow-on studies and books including *Why CEO's Fail* by David Dotlich and Peter Cairo, and *Why Smart Executives Fail* by Sydney Finkelstein.

[9] Crowe, A. (2016). *Alpha project managers: what the top 2% know that everyone else does not (reprint edition)*. Kennesaw, GA: Velociteach. This book was based on a landmark survey of 5,000 project managers and stakeholders; it uncovered and explored eight major areas where top performers stood apart from everyone else.

[10] Thomas, J., Delisle, C., & Jugdev, K. (2002.) *Selling project management to senior executives*. Newtown Square, PA: Project Management Institute. This research study examined why it is hard to get executives and project managers on the same side regarding the value of project management.

[11] Note that the definition and purpose of power that I offer in this book is for positive good, for achieving project results. I am not advocating for the use of power for personal or organizational political gain.

[12] French, J., & Raven, B. (1959). The bases of social power. *Studies in Social Power,* D. Cartwright, Ed., pp. 259-269. Ann Arbor, MI: Institute for Social Research. In a subsequent work, a sixth informational power base was added.

[13] Kotter, J. (1985). *Power and influence: beyond formal authority.* New York, NY: Free Press. This book described how to develop sufficient resources of unofficial power and influence to achieve goals, steer clear of conflicts, foster creative team behavior, and gain the cooperation and support needed from subordinates, co-workers, superiors, and even people outside the organization.

[14] Nye, J. (2005). *Soft power.* New York, NY: Public Affairs Publishing. The author coined the term "soft power" and defined it as the ability to attract and persuade.

[15] O'Brochta, M. (2016, February). Ethics and project success. *ProjectManagement.com.* Retrieved January 22, 2018, from https://www.projectmanagement.com/articles/318380/Ethics-and-Project-Success. The author served on the PMI Ethics Member Advisory Group for seven years, including two years as Chair. This volunteer group was responsible for developing the *PMI Code of Ethics and Professional Conduct* and the *PMI Ethical Decision Making Framework*, both available in a dozen languages.

[16] Kouzes, B., & Posner, B. (2017). *The leadership challenge (sixth edition).* San Francisco, CA: Jossey-Bass. The authors delved into the fundamental roles great leaders fulfill.

[17] Project Management Institute. (2007). PMI Code of Ethics and Professional Conduct. *Project Management Institute.* Retrieved January 22, 2018, from http://www.pmi.org/-/media/pmi/documents/public/pdf/ethics/pmi-code-of-ethics.pdf?sc_lang_temp=en. This document is available in a dozen languages.

[18] Pinto, J. (1998). *Power & politics in project management.* Newtown Square, PA: Project Management Institute. The author included a short list of implications: understand and acknowledge the political nature of most organizations, learn to cultivate appropriate political tactics, understand and accept WIIFM, learn the fine art of influencing, develop negotiating skills, and accept that conflict is a natural side effect.

[19] PricewaterhouseCoopers. (2012). *Insights and trends: current portfolio, programme, and project management practices.* London, UK: PricewaterhouseCoopers. The study included 38 countries. Poor estimation during the planning phase was identified as the largest contributor to project failure; lack of executive sponsorship was second.

[20] Englund, R., & Bucero, A. (2015). *Project sponsorship (second edition).* San Francisco, CA: Jossey-Bass. The authors advocated for a formally established project sponsor role.

[21] Project Management Institute. (2014). *Pulse of the profession: executive sponsor engagement.* Newtown Square, PA: Project Management Institute. This global survey publication reported that the role of executive sponsors has grown by 76% in importance over the past five years and that executive sponsors are in short supply and frequently overextended 84% of the time.

[22] Campbell, G. (2007, October). *Managing senior executives.* PMI Global Congress 2007, Atlanta, GA. The author addressed how to get the right project support from the right level at the right time.

[23] Crawford, J. (2010). *The strategic project office (second edition).* New York, NY: CRC Press. The first edition of this book was selected as the PMI 2001 book of the year; its author previously served as president and chairman of PMI. Other notable books on this subject include *The Advanced Project Management Office* by Parviz Rad and Ginger Levin, *Creating the Project Office* by Randy Englund and Robert Graham, *Building Project Management Centers of Excellence* by Dennis Bolles, and more recently *Leading Successful PMOs* by Peter Taylor.

Chapter 6

WHAT IT TAKES

"Knowledge without action is insanity and action without knowledge is vanity."
Abu al-Ghazali 1882-1946
Theologian

Progress Is Incremental and Cumulative

Progress when it comes to getting executives to act for project success is incremental. The reality is that it does not come all at once, and it does not occur in all organizational elements or in all executives of the organization at the same pace. Since by definition we are dealing with organizational behavior and change, we must recognize that we are dealing with what is usually a slow evolution rather than a sudden revolution. After six editions in print, *Reframing Organizations[1]* has become an accepted standard for categorizing organizational change. This publication identifies the four frames of change as structural, human resource, political, and symbolic. It recognizes that the magnitude of enacting organizational change in any one of these areas is significant. Trying to enact change in multiple areas, as presented in this book, can be substantial. Executives and organizations have spent years becoming who they are. I have found that shifting organization processes and behavior can be particularly challenging; bureaucratic drag can slow or derail even the best of efforts. The good news is that when organizational change does occur, it often builds upon and reinforces itself in a cumulative and enduring way.

Willpower

Knowing what to do and actually doing it are two different things as portrayed in Figure 6.1. In the Alpha study, virtually all project managers were familiar with the concept of project planning, yet it was the Alphas who actually planned twice as much as the others. The others were not disciplined enough. "It is my experience that most project managers are not willing to make

Figure 6.1 – Knowing Doing

the tough and unpopular project-related decisions, even though their instincts warn them that they are not taking the most effective action," says Neal Whitten, one of today's most listened to modern-day project management gurus.[2] Similarly, Jim Collins, one of today's most highly regarded business experts, reports that "an absolutely iron will" is essential in moving from good to great.[3] You can understand, after reading this book, the steps to take as a project manager to help your executive overcome the barriers to take actions for project success. I believe that there is an important factor necessary for you to translate your understanding into results. That factor is willpower.

Willpower is having the discipline to do what is already known to work. Project management willpower is what propels us to resist the pressure and to resist the conflicting forces. Project management willpower is about applying the common sense we have developed with uncommon discipline.[4]

In addition to business and project management gurus, PMI sponsored research has also shown a direct link between the project manager's leadership style and the success of the project, and it has shown that success is more likely when strong willpower-related competencies are demonstrated.[5] In that study, which involved organizations in eight countries, the researchers found that projects dealing with complexity and projects that caused considerable change were more likely to succeed when the project manager had strong emotional competencies related to willpower. In another PMI sponsored study, project success was positively correlated to project managers who had the discipline to emphasize a transformational leadership style that focused on the inspiration and motivation of project team members even when confronted with organizational and cultural resistance.[6] Interestingly, one project management certification includes a competency related to willpower. The Federal Acquisition Certification for Program and Project Managers (FAC-P/PM), which is available to U.S. Government employees, includes the willpower-related competency of resilience.[7]

Unfortunately, for many of us, willpower is in short supply and seems hard to develop. Apparently, it is our brain's fault. According to a feature story in *Time Magazine*,[8] "Pity your prefrontal cortex, the CEO and chief justice of the bedlam that is your brain. It's the prefrontal that has to reconcile the artiste of your right hemisphere with the logician of your left, the tough guy of your hypothalamus with the drama queen of your anterior cingulate cortex." Evidently, we are wired to do certain activities, such as eat when we can rather than when we need to, and we are wired to give preference to short-term pleasures over long-term sacrifices. Neuroscience use of functional magnetic resonance imaging reveals that our brains have an "imbalance between the restraint and indulgence systems." This fact could unhelpfully provide us some comfort in claiming, "it is not my fault if I failed to have the discipline to use my willpower to perform project management basic steps."

Worse yet, it appears that even if we are able to exert willpower in one area, that often leads to backsliding in other areas. In one of the most widely cited studies in social science, we learn what happens when people followed instructions to use their willpower to suppress their emotions during the showing of a sad movie.[9] "Either way, the effort to control their emotional reactions depleted their willpower. Faking it didn't come free." Willpower tires us out in many different ways, including "resisting food or drink, suppressing emotional responses, restraining aggressive or sexual impulses, taking exams, and trying to impress someone." Additionally, critically important for project managers is "Task persistence is also reduced." That strikes at the very heart of successful project management. Performing tasks, especially those that have been identified as needed steps to overcoming the barriers for executives to take action for project, is what is being called for.

In the short term we can spend our limited willpower budget wisely. For example, if you want to be capable of drawing on your full supply of willpower for an important step toward executive action, then you would not spend time immediately prior to that step engaged in a task you found arduous; you would save your willpower reserve for when it was most important.

For the long term, breakthrough research is now showing us that willpower can be built and strengthened.[10] I think this represents a key to unlocking the potential so many project managers have developed as they have gained skills and knowledge. This key can be used by project managers to allow them to apply the common sense they are developing with uncommon discipline. As revealed in this breakthrough research, we find that our brains already include the willpower muscle, and it is used every day. And like a muscle, willpower can be strengthened. Researchers are learning what kind of calisthenics it takes to get our willpower into shape. First and foremost is the discipline of routine and habit. In psychological studies, even something as simple as using your non-dominant hand to brush your teeth for two weeks can increase willpower capacity. People who stick to an exercise program for two months report reducing their impulsive spending, junk food intake, alcohol use, and smoking. They also study more, watch less television, and do more housework. Other forms of willpower training, like money-management classes, work as well. Strengthening willpower in one area builds willpower strength in other areas.

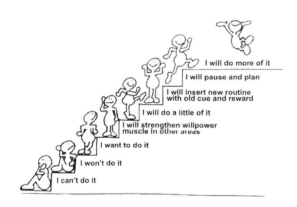

Figure 6.2 – Strengthen Willpower

Even a small change to a routine, if repeated often enough, will evolve into a new habit as illustrated in Figure 6.2. Since more than forty percent of the actions we perform each day are not the product of deliberate actions but of habit, we need only to develop a couple of new habits.[11] The key to habit change is to keep the old cue signal that leads you to the old reward but to insert a new routine in place of the old one. "If getting home from work is usually a cue to flop onto the couch and munch chips while watching TV, put a pair of laced-up sneakers by the front door. Substitute a new routine, an early-evening run, for the old one of snacking, but keep the reward; after exercising, allow yourself to watch your favorite show. Repeat this often enough, and you will have a habit you want to keep."

During this strengthening of the willpower muscle, lapsing back to the old ways can be a constant temptation; a pause-and-plan strategy can help.[12] When temptations arise to deviate from the new habit, the urge to give in can be strong: "It won't hurt to skip this one step toward executive action." The mind's focus is narrowed on the temptation; this narrowing leaves few options other than to give in. However, those temptations can be circumvented with a little effort in advance. Pausing and planning well in advance of the temptation crisis widens the options and brings the rational prefrontal cortex further into play.

Forgiveness works too. After we inevitably experience an occasional lapse, berating or shaming ourselves into getting back on course may be counterproductive. Willpower research found those who forgave themselves for failing at a task were more likely to brush themselves off and try again.[13] It was demonstrated that dieters given a pep talk after eating a doughnut, emphasizing that one small setback would not ruin all their hard efforts, were less likely to indulge later on than doughnut eaters who did not have the talk. "If we want to have more willpower, we have to learn to be a friend and mentor to ourselves, rather than equating self-control with self-criticism.

Adding a new project management basic to your routine will, if it does not require too much extra effort, evolve into a standard behavior. Small increments accomplished over a period of time will produce notable increases in willpower, similar to the progression experienced by someone starting a new physical fitness program. This progression of willpower strengthening, can move the project manager from old habit to new.

Barriers exist to achieving the level of willpower necessary for project managers to take the steps needed to get executives to act for project success; our brains are wired differently, and we backslide. In the short term, we can spend our limited willpower budget wisely. For the long term, breakthrough research is now showing us that willpower can be built and strengthened. Strengthening willpower in one area builds willpower strength in other areas. Changing habits to strengthen willpower involves keeping the old cue signal that leads to the old reward, but inserting a new routine in place of the old one. This is great news. Adding a new project management basic to your routine will evolve into a standard behavior if it does not require too much extra effort, one that contributes to your taking steps to help executives overcome barriers and take actions for project success.

Delayed Gratification

The actions listed in this book for executives to take are long-term, as are the steps identified for you to take to help your executive overcome the barriers to actually take those actions. They are strategic, not tactical. As such, they are more easily accomplished by project managers and executives who are capable of delayed gratification. Generally, delayed gratification is associated with resisting a smaller but more immediate reward in order to receive a larger or more enduring reward later. A person's ability to delay gratification relates to other similar skills, such as patience, impulse control, self-control, and willpower.

Figure 6.3 – Gratification

The seminal research on delayed gratification, the now-famous "marshmallow experiment," was conducted by Walter Mischel in the 1960's and 1970's at Stanford University.[14] Mischel and his colleagues were interested in strategies that preschool children used to resist temptation. They presented four-year-olds with a marshmallow and told the children that they had two options: ring a bell at any point to summon the experimenter and eat the marshmallow, or wait until the experimenter returned about 15 minutes later, and earn two marshmallows as illustrated in Figure 6.3. The message was "small reward now, bigger reward later." Some children broke down and ate the one marshmallow, whereas others were able to delay gratification and earn the coveted two marshmallows. In follow-up experiments, Mischel found that children were able to wait longer if they used certain distraction techniques (such as covering their eyes, hiding under the desk, singing songs, or imagining pretzels instead of the marshmallow in front of them), or if they changed the way they thought about the marshmallow (focusing on its similarity to a cotton ball rather than on its gooey, delectable taste).

The children who waited longer, when re-evaluated as teenagers and adults, demonstrated a striking array of advantages over their peers. As teenagers, they had higher SAT scores, social competence, self-assuredness, and self-worth and were rated by their parents as more mature, better able to cope with stress, more likely to plan ahead, and more likely to use reason. They were less likely to have conduct disorders or high levels of impulsivity, aggressiveness, and hyperactivity. As adults, the high delayers were less likely to have drug problems or other addictive behaviors, get divorced, or become overweight. Each minute that a preschooler was able to delay gratification translated to a 0.2% reduction in Body Mass Index 30 years later. Follow-up studies continued to confirm that the ability to resist temptation early in life translated into persistent benefits.

When you employ the characteristic of delayed gratification, you will enable a sharper focus on your taking the steps to help executives overcome barriers and take actions for project success.

Some Final Thoughts

Thank you, dear reader, for your time and attention. The fact that you invested in this book suggests to me that you are already on the path to getting your executive to act for project success.

My goal was to make this a how-to book, one where there were explanations for the included actions and steps. I explored why the evolving and expanding definition of project success and why the expanding complexity and number of projects have led to an environment in which the project manager is ever more dependent on the executive. Then, I identified executive actions most likely to contribute to project success. And, I gave repeated emphasis to the benefits of a strong mutual partnership between project managers and executives and to the success not only of your own projects and careers, but also to the success of others and to the success of the organization in which you work.

I explored the barriers likely to confront your executive, described a number of steps you can take as a project manager to help your executive overcome those barriers so he or she can actually take the actions needed for project success, and I provided a model so you can gauge levels of executive support for projects. I described progress as being incremental and cumulative and linked the characteristics of willpower and delayed gratification to your long-term strategic goals to get executives to take action for project success.

I employed a central theme which recognized that you are empowered to extend your sphere of power beyond the immediate project boundaries up into the organization, not only to get your executives to act, but also to help implement the actions as well. Finally, I included an appendix written for executives that presents the essential elements of this book in a form and tone that has been tailored to their needs. You can provide that appendix to your executive as part of your building of a strong mutual partnership focused on the executive actions for project success.

Chapter End Notes

[1] Bolman, L., & Deal, T. (2017). *Reframing organizations: artistry, choice, and leadership (sixth edition)*. San Francisco, CA: Jossey-Bass. The authors combined the latest research from organizational theory, organizational behavior, psychology, sociology, and political science and provided insight into the organizational culture.

---

[2] Whitten, N. (2005). *No-nonsense advice for successful projects.* Vienna, VA: Management Concepts Press. This popular author, mentor, and speaker distilled experience gained working with thousands of project managers across hundreds of companies and projects.

[3] Collins, J. (2001). *Good to great.* New York, NY: HarperCollins. The author reported study results that identified the benefits of a culture of discipline.

[4] I bought into the value of willpower and discipline years ago, professionally and personally. In 2003 it saved my life and the lives of the other members of our climbing team. When confronted with a brutally unforgiving storm while ascending Mt. Aconcagua, the highest mountain in the world outside of the Himalayan range, we exercised discipline to stop ascending beyond our predetermined turn-around time. Seven others from a different climbing team, who did not exercise this level of discipline, died.

[5] Turner, J., & Muller, R. (2006). *Choosing appropriate project managers – matching their leadership style to the type of project.* Newtown Square, PA: Project Management Institute. The authors reported on research conducted into the relationship between leadership style and the performance of organizations and projects.

[6] Reilly, R. (2007). *The human side of project leadership.* Newtown Square, PA: Project Management Institute. This collection of three academic articles related to the human side of project management illuminated the ways in which leadership, project spirit, and conflict management skills impact project success.

[7] Federal Acquisition Institute. (2013). *FAC-P/PM Competencies/Aligned Skills.* Retrieved January 22, 2018, from https://www.fai.gov/drupal/sites/default/files/2013-9-23-PPM-Competency-Model.pdf. This project competency model, which I helped to develop, identified a full set of leadership traits that included resilience.

[8] Kluger, J. (2012). Getting to no – the Science of Building Willpower. *Time Magazine 179(9) 42-47.* This attention-grabbing article captured some of the current thinking about willpower.

[9] Baumeister, R., & Tierney, J. (2012). *Willpower: rediscovering the greatest human strength.* New York, NY: Penguin Books. The pioneering researcher Roy F. Baumeister collaborated with renowned *New York Times* science writer John Tierney to revolutionize our understanding of the most coveted human virtue: self-control.

[10] McGonigal, K. (2011). *The willpower instinct: how self-control works, why it matters, and what you can do to get more of it.* New York, NY: Avery. Informed by the latest research and combining cutting-edge insights from psychology, economics, neuroscience, and medicine, the author explained exactly what willpower is, how it works, and why it matters.

[11] Duhigg, C. (2012). *The power of habit: why we do what we do in life and business.* New York, NY: Random House. The award-winning *New York Times* business reporter took the reader to the thrilling edge of scientific discoveries to explain why habits exist and how they can be changed.

[12] Segerstrom, S., Hardey, J., Evans, D., & Winters, N. (2011). Pause and pain: self-regulation and the heart. *In R. Wright & G. Gendolla (Eds.), Motivational perspectives on cardiovascular response* (pp 181-198). Washington, DC: American Psychological Association. Academic treatment of the process for moving forward when confronted with physiological pain.

[13] Baumeister, R., & Tierney, J. (2012). *Willpower: rediscovering the greatest human strength.* New York, NY: Penguin Books. The pioneering researcher Roy F. Baumeister collaborated with renowned *New York Times* science writer John Tierney to revolutionize our understanding of the most coveted human virtue: self-control.

[14] Mischel, W., Shoda, Y, & Rodriguez, M. (1989). Delay of Gratification in Children. *Science,* New Series, Vol. 244, No 4907 (May 26, 1989), 933-938. American Association of Science. Forty years after the first marshmallow test studies, neuroimaging data shed light on the neural correlates of delayed gratification. 59 of the original participants, who were in their mid-40s, were given a delayed gratification task. Those who had been high delayers as preschoolers were more successful at controlling their impulse responses later in life.

Appendix

This appendix has been written for executives. It presents the essential elements of this book in a form and tone that has been tailored to their needs.

For Executives

Projects matter. They deliver benefits to customers and to the organization. As an executive, you are challenged by working in an environment in which your organization's success is strongly tied to the success of the projects within your organization. You are challenged to contribute actively to the success of the projects within your organization. But how can you take action for that project success? This topic has resonated strongly with the thousands of project managers and executives whom I have had the pleasure of addressing directly, as well as with the even greater numbers of people who have reacted to articles I have written about this topic in business and project management publications.

The good news for you as an executive is that you can take proven actions toward project success, and by doing so, you can raise the odds of your organization's success. In this appendix you will

- Learn why your organization's success is now more dependent on project success
- Find out what proven actions you can take for project success
- Recognize the barriers to your actions
- See how your project managers can employ familiar management approaches to help you overcome these barriers.

Why Are Executives Important?

Projects matter. They deliver benefits to customers and to the organization. Projects enable an organization to accomplish its strategic goals. Projects enable the executive to succeed. But projects often fail; organizations fail. So, too, do executives.

Who cares? Both executives and project managers, that is who. One reason the topic of acting for project success seems to get so much traction is the convergence of mutual interests between executives, who are working to implement their strategic vision, and project managers, who have an extraordinary focus on delivering results. A June 1999 *Fortune Magazine* article reported that the number one reason executives fail is "bad execution. As simple as that: not getting things done, being indecisive, not delivering on commitments."

I believe that executives who are working to avoid this type of failure are well served by recognizing and embracing their dependency on project management. You as a executive are in an environment in which work is, with increasing frequency, being conducted as projects with more and more employees are using project management methods. According to the Project Management Institute, the world's leading project-management professional organization, membership and credential holders have doubled in just the past few years to more than 470,000 people worldwide in over 200 countries.

The logic seems inescapable to me: You as a executive are being measured by your ability to deliver organizational results. Because project management is almost entirely about delivering results, your needs are well-served by, even dependent on, project success. Execution matters to your business and to you.

Just as your success is increasingly dependent on the outcome of projects, project success has become increasingly dependent on you the executive. This is where significant opportunities for executive action exist and are desperately needed. According to a global survey on the state of project management, conducted by PricewaterhouseCoopers in 2012, "lack of executive sponsorship was the second largest factor that contributed to poor project performance." A broader worldwide survey conducted by Towers Perrin, a global workforce services company, revealed that three-quarters of the employees surveyed "said that their organizations or senior management do not do enough to help them fully engage and contribute to their organization's success."

Project managers have found that project success has become more difficult to achieve in recent years. Projects are more complex, their scope has broadened, and the very definition of success has expanded. In the early days of project management, success was measured predominantly in technical terms. Projects either worked, or they did not. Today, project success has many more dimensions: technical, cost, schedule, customer satisfaction, impact on other projects, and strategic impact on the organization. This new nature of projects has made project managers more dependent on their executives for project success.

Project managers are seriously seeking your support as an executive, and in most places, they are not finding it. They are chomping at the bit for executive action. This is a terrific opportunity for you the executive to step forward and take action.

What Can Executives Do To Act For Project Success?

Are you an executive who:

- Leads an organization that depends on projects and on project managers?

- Is motivated to identify and overcome the barriers to project success?

- Understands the strong relationship between project success and the success of your organization's strategic objectives, not to mention your own personal success?

- Wants to make a bigger impact on your organization?

If so, there is good news. The executive actions for project success are largely known and understood. They have been proven to work. Project management practitioners have been engaged for quite some time in identifying the actions that they would like their executives to take for project success. Figure A-1 lists proven executive actions for project success that you can readily adapt, then adopt. This list has stood the test of time. It is based on my own experiences in project management working with thousands of project managers and with executives at the Central Intelligence Agency and elsewhere, and it is based on a considerable number of publications and studies from leading authors and organizations.

Organize And Manage Work As Projects; Pick The Right Projects

The most essential executive actions are *organize and manage work as projects* and *pick the right projects*. Project managers can feel like fish out of water when they work in an environment that is not structured around projects. Much effort can be spent trying to educate and convince the myriad stakeholders about the merits of the project process basics. Discussions and disagreement can occur about the amount of planning, the completeness of requirements definition, the use of baselines and change management, schedule precision, and the criteria for accepting a project deliverable. Most certainly, these are necessary discussions. However, each time they occur, they draw time and resources away from the actual management of the project. Importantly, they limit the odds of project success. Study findings in a recent *PMI Pulse of the Profession* report indicate that projects are 2.5 times more successful when repeatable project management practices are used. It is far more efficient to have these discussions once, establish and document a standardized project management process, and be accountable for following that process. Then, over time, as the project managers and the executives gain experience with the standardized process, that process can be suitably tailored for each individual project, and it can be incrementally improved.

It is easy for project managers to become overwhelmed if they have too many projects to work on. That is why it is essential to pick the right projects. The project selection method can be sophisticated as strategic portfolio management or as simple as choosing only projects the project managers and project teams have the capacity to perform. Either way, the goal is to identify a limited number of top priority projects. Consider the reality when too many projects are ranked the number one priority; in reality none of them is.

I favor the simple approach: do only as many projects as can be done well and do not agonize too much over the decisions about which projects to undertake. Do not overtask the project manager. Actual research into the optimum number of projects for a project manager to manage successfully is sparse; however, fewer projects are better; fewer projects mean

WHAT TO DO

☐ **Organize And Manage Work As Projects**

☐ **Pick The Right Projects**

☐ **Maintain Close Stakeholder Relationships**

☐ **Use Suitable Project Management Process**

☐ **Ensure Projects Follow Documented Plan**

☐ **Ensure Projects Are Based On Requirements**

☐ **Ensure Resources Are Sufficient**

☐ **Engage Middle Management Help**

☐ **Use Job Performance Standards**

☐ **Make And Support Timely Decisions**

☐ **Ask The Right Questions**

Figure A.1 – Executive Actions

more time spent per project. Although counterintuitive for some, fewer projects mean that ultimately more projects conclude successfully. Since successful projects do not overrun budgets or schedules, money and time become available for other projects.

Maintain Close Stakeholder Relationships

Executives have a unique responsibility to develop and *maintain close stakeholder relationships* that complement and enhance the relationships formed by the project manager. The time invariably comes when an issue, concern, or decision must be addressed by someone other than the project manager. This type of supportive intervention is often helpful when decisions about project funding, priority, and requirements must be made.

Note that these executive relationships should be conducted in such a way that the project manager's authority and responsibility are maintained, and the project manager is kept in the loop and well informed. Ideally, the project manager should bring issues to the attention of the executive.

Use Suitable Project Management Process

Project management is a discipline and, as such, benefits from adhering to a *suitable project management process*. Project managers who are at the top of their game have come to rely on executives to establish a standardized process for their organization to use. They seek to be held accountable for applying tailored versions of this process to each of their projects. They can, in the absence of executive action, develop and follow their own processes, but they recognize the limits in efficiency and effectiveness of doing so. For project managers, there is freedom through suitable process. According to a recent *PMI Pulse of the Profession* report, for organizations, the use of a suitable standard process increases project success rates by 23%.

Ensure Projects Follow Documented Plan; Ensure Projects Are Based On Requirements

Project managers expect executives to ensure that they *follow a documented project plan* and that *projects are based on documented requirements*. They expect you to give them adequate time up front during the initial project phase to build these baseline documents. They should not be pressured to proceed hastily without them. This expectation applies not only for predictive life cycles (such as waterfall), but also for iterative, incremental, and adaptive (such as agile) life cycles. Project managers also expect you to hold them accountable for continuous, controlled revisions to these documents through the project life cycle.

Planning and requirements are the foundation for project management, and their level of importance cannot be overstated. Virtually every set of project performance statistics I have examined during the past couple of decades lists inadequate planning and inadequate requirements as the leading causes of project failure. Additionally, it is expensive to shortchange planning and requirements. A NASA study found that the cost of fixing a requirements error late in the life cycle during the operations phase was about 1,000 times greater than if that error had been fixed during the up-front requirements phase; other industries have comparably large multipliers.

Ensure Resources Are Sufficient; Engage Middle Management Help

Project managers expect their executives to ensure that the *project resources* they receive (time, people, and money) are *sufficient*. If shortages or changes occur, the project manager should not be pressured simply to absorb the effects of the change or do more with less. He or she should give the executive an impact assessment that explains the effects of the shortage or change. That impact assessment then serves as the basis for revisions to the baseline plans, requirements, and other documents.

Engaging middle management can be a powerful bottom-up and top-down step executives can take toward project success. Since middle managers are closer to the projects and project managers than the executives are, they have the opportunity for a significant amount of bottom-up insight into the needs of those projects and project managers.

Use Job Performance Standards

Project managers, especially those who are in it for the long-term, are interested in working in an established career path with *established job performance standards*. They view project management as highly personal, as a way of life, as a way of making a living, and as a challenge of their capabilities that can provide deep satisfaction. These project managers understand that the outcome of their projects plays a significant role in their career advancement, and they understand the value of being evaluated against a common set of competency-based job performance standards. According to a recent talent management study, organizations using established job standards realize a substantial increase in project success rates.

Make And Support Timely Decisions

Successful project managers have learned the benefits of identifying and managing against the critical path, the sequence of project activities that determine the shortest completion time. Any delay, for whatever reason, in the critical path, will delay project completion and/or negatively impact the project cost and scope. Consequently, project managers are looking to their executives to *make timely decisions.*

Ask The Right Questions

This is my favorite executive action for project success. It speaks to the strong mutual partnership between you the executive and the project manager that is central to acting for project success. It also speaks to the difference between your roles and responsibilities and that of the project manager. *Asking the right questions,* as shown in Figure A.2, can help you minimize the tempting distraction to get too far into the project details, to solve the project issues, to get ahead of the schedule, or to encroach on doing the project manager's job.

At the top of the list is perhaps the most effective question for the executive to ask the project manager: "What can I do to help?" The effectiveness of this question has repeatedly been demonstrated during the forty years since it was first associated with the groundbreaking servant leadership approach by Robert Greenleaf into the nature of power and greatness. It places the executive in a position to support the project manager while at the same time holding him or her accountable for his or her responsibilities and commitments.

What can I do to help?

What do you think?

What are the requirements?

What is the plan?

What are the top risks?

What is the status?

What is the stakeholder's view?

What is the impact?

What is the basis?

Figure A.2 – Questions

What Are The Executive Barriers?

It is essential to acknowledge that you likely cannot accomplish all of the actions on the list. Even those executives predisposed to action will find that their circumstances and the pressures of their jobs make it difficult at best to accomplish but so many actions for project success.

Viewpoints Differ; Project Management Knowledge Differs

Your executive's viewpoint differs from that of the project manager. Whereas project managers tend to view project management quite personally, often with little or no distinction between their performance and the performance of the project, executives tend to view project management as a means to an end, as a good way of motivating people toward achievement of specific objectives, as a source of future executives, and as a means to achieve strategic objectives. On the negative side, project managers can see project management as a source of considerable frustration as they attempt to execute their responsibilities in the face of inadequate authority, misunderstanding, skepticism, and occasionally even hostile attitudes. Similarly negative, executives can see project management as an unsettling and possibly disruptive influence on the traditional organization, a necessary evil, a threat to their established authority, a cause for unwanted change to the status quo, and unwanted evidence of deficiencies or failures in the traditional functional organization.

Although project management may be second nature for project managers, that is unlikely to be the case for you as an executive. A recent article in *CIO Magazine* by former Project Management Institute Chairman Antonio Nieto-Rodriguez suggests a couple of likely reasons. He points out that in the *Harvard Business Review*, one of the gold standards for sources of business management thinking for almost one hundred years, fewer than one-half of one percent of the published articles have been about project management. Likewise for business management education, only two of the top one hundred MBA programs in the world teach project management as a core course. Given this lack of attention in business publications and lack of attention in business schools, it should come as no surprise that 80% of project management executives do not know how their projects align with their organization's business strategy or that one-third of all project failures are attributed to a lack of executive involvement. I certainly do not advocate for executives to learn to be project managers. However, I do advocate for executives to recognize this knowledge gap and to act accordingly.

Change Readiness Level; Organizational Maturity

Executives and organizations are at varying levels of change readiness. It does little good to push for a change if you and/or the organization are not ready; in fact, it is counterproductive and "sours the well water" for future attempts. High readiness levels are characterized by strong desires for change and readiness for it; a strong resistance to change characterizes low readiness levels. Moderate readiness levels are characterized by a desire for change but a lack of readiness. For example, if there were a merger yesterday, and if there is a reorganization today, then tomorrow would not be a good time for an executive to try to implement a substantial change to the organization's standard project life cycle. A more appropriate executive action would be to grant approval for a single project to tailor the standard life cycle in a way that benefits the project but does not broadly impact other projects and processes in the organization. The larger organization-wide change can wait.

The volume of work, important work, that is already within the executive's domain is significant. Time and resources for carrying out these actions for project success may be very limited. Additionally, your organization will itself impose limitations on what can be done. Your organization's level of maturity limits what it is capable of accomplishing even if the necessary time and resources are available. If your organization's projects are characterized by last-minute heroics, ad-hoc activity, and a lack of formal processes, you should choose only an item or two from the list of executive actions. By contrast, executives who work in organizations with well-defined, repeatable processes that undergo continuous improvement have the latitude to undertake a greater number of items on the list.

Organizational Politics; Limited Authority

People, after all, are at the center of your work life. And, in organizations where there are people, there is politics. Organizational politics can subvert even a well-intentioned executive's action for project success in favor of the politically expedient. The field of project management, in particular, is fraught with politics, in large part because the ability to get things done is invariably shared among numerous entities. Additionally, the vast majority of projects exist outside of the traditional organizational structure in a matrix configuration where executives and project managers are relegated to the role of supernumerary. Neither the executive nor the project manager has the sufficient levels of formal authority needed for project success. Add to this the cast of characters with roles as project stakeholders, and competing agendas invariably come into play. In a study reported in the *Academy of Management Journal*, 93% of executives surveyed reported that workplace politics exists in their organization, and 70% felt that in order to be successful, a person has to engage in politics. It was a leading source for conflicting executive demands.

From the project manager's viewpoint, it might be easy for him or her to see you as someone with a sizeable amount of authority, especially relative to their own. Indeed, that may be the case in some situations. However, according to business guru and best-selling author Michael Porter, it is far more likely that the levels of your authority fall short of what is needed for you to take actions for project success. Even though you may bear full responsibility for the organization's well-being, you are apt to be a few steps removed from many of the factors needed to take those actions. Position and title alone do not confer the authority to lead. For example, it might be difficult for an executive to mandate the use of a standard project life cycle on projects in his or her element of the organization if a number of the project team members on those projects are matrixed from other elements in the organization that follow different life cycle methodologies. A more appropriate action might be to resolve the conflicts of authority for those project team members before addressing a standard project life cycle.

What Steps Can Project Managers Take To Help You?

A key message for project managers is to look for opportunities to help you overcome executive barriers so that you can take the actions needed for project success. Project managers recognize the benefits of forming a strong mutual partnership with you the executive. Steps that they are prepared to take, as listed in Figure A.3, include developing the ability to communicate effectively the value of successful projects by using business terms and by establishing and growing sufficient power to be heeded.

Speak Truth To Power

Because recent research reported in the *Harvard Business Review* reveals that executives simply do not appreciate how risky it can feel for others to speak up, project managers are prepared to learn how to effectively speak truth to power. Their speaking must be wholly truthful, devoid of self-interest, without harming any innocents, and without spite or anger; authenticity is key. Project managers must, first and foremost, know their facts, state their case, respectfully stand their ground, keep their cool, and offer you options. And, one of the most effective options is for them to offer you help.

Speak Truth To Power

Emphasize Value Of Successful Projects

Behave Like An Alpha

Communicate Using Business Context

Understand And Use Power

Leverage Sponsors And Champions

Form A Project Management Council

Use Executive Actions List

Figure A.3 – PM Steps

Emphasize Value Of Successful Projects

Once the project manager has established an effective means to speak to you the executive, he or she can undertake the process of helping you understand the contribution successful projects and mature project management practices make to that bottom line. Study findings in a recent *PMI Pulse of the Profession* report showed that projects within organizations that adhere to proven project management practices meet original goals and business intent 90% of the time versus only 36% of the time for organizations not adhering to proven project management practices. Furthermore, those organizations using proven project management practices wasted about 13 times less money than the low performers. The report points out that one of the significant contributors to the remarkably better performance of the organizations using proven project management practices is the attention they pay to aligning their projects to the organizational strategy and goals.

Behave Like An Alpha

A survey of over 5,000 project managers, stakeholders, and executives has provided an extraordinary insight into what the top two percent of project managers know and do that everyone else does not. This is one of my favorite studies of all time because it gets to the heart of successful project management. Armed with this information, your project managers can take steps to be more effective in their jobs, which in turn should move their bona fides in a direction where you will be more inclined to appreciate the information and action requests they bring to you.

This study focused on identifying the best project managers, referred to as Alpha project managers, and then on determining what they did that made them the best. Opinions about these project managers were obtained from team members, customers, and executives. The study results revealed large differences between what the Alpha project managers believe and do versus the non-Alpha project managers. The Alphas were found to believe strongly that they had enough authority to manage the project, 89 percent for Alphas vs. 49 percent for non-Alphas. The Alphas also distinguished themselves when planning projects. Although the study revealed both Alphas and non-Alphas understood equally the importance of planning, the Alphas dedicated double the amount of project time to actually planning. And, the Alphas distinguished themselves when communicating. Both Alphas and non-Alphas equally understood the value of communication; however, the Alphas were viewed by others as being much more effective at performing the actual communication, 80% for Alphas vs. 49% for non-Alphas.

Communicate Using Business Context

How project managers communicate with you as an executive has at least as much effect as what they communicate. Even a well-crafted project management message will fall flat if you fail to hear it. Consequently, project managers are prepared to take steps to communicate with you using business context. The findings from a research study involving two thousand project personnel, consultants, and executives reveal that effective communication between project manager and executive begins long before the message is passed; it begins by building a relationship first. Once that is achieved, this excellent body of work instructs project managers to emphasize alignment of project management and project goals with corporate goals and value statements. It identifies the value of using business language and putting the project in context of business value where project aspects that relate to financial, growth, customer satisfaction, competition, and sales are emphasized.

Understand And Use Power; Leverage Sponsors And Champions; Form A Project Management Council

The degree that project managers are listened to when speaking to executives is, to some degree, related to the amount of organizational power they possess. Power refers to the ability of project managers to influence you and others to act for the benefit of their projects. This is a relatively new topic for most project managers because while they can easily see your sources of power, few of them have discovered or developed their own power sources.

They are now recognizing that they have a considerable source of expert power that is centered around what they know about their project. They are now recognizing that they also have referent power, based on their many affiliations across the organization. Both of these sources of power can grow or be short circuited, depending on the project manager's level of trust and ethical behavior. Because as reported in *The Leadership Challenge*, a best seller after six editions and 20 years in print, "It's clear that if people anywhere are to willingly follow someone, whether it be into battle or into the boardroom, the front office or the front lines, they first want to assure themselves that the person is worthy of their trust."

In an effort to grow their expert and referent power, project managers understand that if one project management voice is good, two voices are better, and a group of voices is even better. Consequently, they are prepared to form a project management council, a small group of like-minded project managers focused on how project management is, can, and should be practiced within the organization.

Use Executive Actions List

Project managers are preparing to blend their experience and judgment, to reflect upon the unique circumstances of their project and the organization, and to solicit from their fellow project managers in order to tailor and use the *Executive Actions List.* That tailoring will reflect the reality of what can be achieved in your organization at this point in time, and it will take into account barriers to executive action.

What Does It Take Succeed?

Progress, when it comes to getting you the executive to act for project success, is typically incremental. It does not come all at once, and it does not occur in all elements or in all executives of the organization at the same pace. Since by definition we are dealing with organizational behavior and change, we must recognize we are dealing with what is usually a slow evolution rather than a sudden revolution. The good news it that when organizational change does occur, it often builds upon and reinforces itself in a cumulative and enduring way.

Willpower

It is useful for project managers and executives to recognize that knowing what to do and actually doing it are two different things. "It is my experience that most project managers are not willing to make the tough and unpopular project-related decisions, even though their instincts warn them that they are not taking the most effective action," says Neal Whitten, one of today's most listened to, modern-day project management gurus. Willpower is needed. Willpower is having the discipline to do what is already known to work. Project management willpower is what propels us to resist the pressure and to resist the conflicting forces. Project management willpower is about applying the common sense project managers have developed with uncommon discipline. Fortunately, breakthrough research is now showing us that willpower can be built and strengthened.

Delayed Gratification

The actions listed in this book for you the executive to take are long-term as are the steps identified for project managers to take to help you overcome the barriers to actually take those actions. They are strategic, not tactical. As such, they are more easily accomplished by project managers and executives who are capable of delayed gratification. Generally, delayed gratification is associated with resisting a smaller but more immediate reward in order to receive a larger or more enduring reward later. A person's ability to delay gratification relates to other similar skills such as patience, impulse control, self-control, and willpower.

Some Final Thoughts

I have presented what I think is a good-news story to you the executive:. You can promote project success by taking action. Together, we have examined the critical dependency between executive success and project success. I have

- Listed proven executive actions for project success and encouraged you to adapt the list by seeking the advice of project managers in your organization

- Acknowledged the barriers that may make it challenging for you the executive to implement these actions

- Discussed steps project managers can take to help you to break down these barriers

- Advocated for the value of willpower and delayed gratification

- Strongly encouraged you and your project managers to work together to form a strong mutual partnership.

Exercises

These exercises are provided to help readers advance to higher levels of learning and to assist readers in applying the information in this book. These exercises, which are keyed to the book chapters, can be performed individually or together with other members of the reader's organization.

Exercise 2.1

Objective

Identify underlying problems associated with a project in an organization.

Become familiar with the case study.

Background

Projects exist in organizations where project success is dependent on executives.

Instructions

Read case study titled "The Fractured Review."

Develop a statement that describes an underlying problem in the case.

Record for use during future exercises.

**Underlying
Problem Statement**

Exercise 3.1

Objective

Identify executive actions for project success.

Background

Project managers are dependent on executive actions for project success.

Instructions

Examine the list of 11 executive actions.

From your previous experience, identify additional executive actions to enable project success; identify what the actions are, why they are important, and how they could be accomplished.

Record for use during future exercises.

**Additional
Executive Actions**

What   Why   How

Exercise 3.2

Objective

Identify executive actions for project success.

Background

Project managers are dependent on executive actions for project success.

Instructions

Read case study titled "The Fractured Review."

Identify the executive actions that could have or can be taken to raise the likelihood of project success; include rationale for each executive action.

Rank order importance into categories: Top and Other.

Record for use during future exercises.

Executive Actions

	Action	Why
Top	_____	_____
	_____	_____
	_____	_____
Other	_____	_____
	_____	_____
	_____	_____

Exercise 4.1

Objective

Identify barriers to executive actions for project success.

Background

Projects exist in organizations where project success is dependent on executives.

Instructions

Read case study titled "The Fractured Review."

For each of the Top actions identified in Exercise 3.2, develop a list of barriers to executive action in the case; include rationale for each executive barrier.

Record for use during future exercises.

Executive Actions

	Action	Barrier
Top		

Exercise 4.2

Objective

Gauge executive support.

Background

Executive support can be gauged using a measurement model.

Instructions

Consider the list of Barriers identified in Exercise 4.1.

Gauge the executive support level by placing an "X" on the *Executive Support For Projects* model.

Record for use during future exercises.

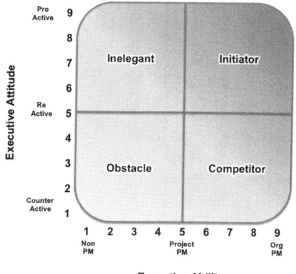

Exercise 5.1

Objective

Identify steps project managers can take to help executives overcome the barriers.

Background

Projects managers are well positioned and motivated to help executives.

Instructions

Read case study titled "The Fractured Review."

For each of the executive barriers identified in Exercise 4.1, develop a list of project management steps to help the executive in the case; include rationale for each project management step.

Record for use.

PM Actions

Top Barrier	PM Action	Why
___	___	___
___	___	___
___	___	___

Case Study

The Fractured Review

The Dynamo project was a development effort to build a hardware version of a signal processor that had been built previously in software. A prime requirement for this hardware version was to maintain the same functionality as the software version while at the same time improving the throughput by a factor of ten. The same people who had been using the software version were eager for the faster hardware version; discussions were already taking place about the potential for building a large quantity of these signal processors. Bill Bronson was the Dynamo project manager, and he viewed the receipt of this assignment with much enthusiasm. He had very much enjoyed the software signal processor development projects he had previously done, looked on this assignment as a reward for his previous successes, and thought it a good opportunity to get some hardware experience on a project low in risk. He was still concentrating on the review he had just completed with his Board of Directors (BOD) for this project when he received a call from June Simmons. June had been one of Bill's longest acquaintances since he joined the System Engineering Division a decade ago. She had spent her career on the operations end of the business as compared to Bill's career choices, which had always kept him on the development end. It was during his phone conversation with June that Bill began to vocalize some of the frustration that had been steadily building.

He related to June how it seemed that little of what he presented at the review was satisfactory to the executives on the BOD. This caught him off guard, at least to some degree, since he tried to follow closely the review templates that he had used for previous projects. On the other hand, perhaps when he was being entirely candid with himself, he could recall similar difficulties with the same BOD during previous Dynamo reviews. In any event, Bill found himself fielding question after question about how the Dynamo algorithms were going to operate at such increased speeds and still maintain their precision. Bill tried at first to deflect these questions by pointing out that the project was still in the concept definition phase and not yet through the design phase. This was interpreted by the BOD to be unresponsive and overly dependent on process when what they really wanted was someone with more technical experience who had the answers. They were acting on their doubts about assigning a software project manager to a hardware project. And, they were acting on the sense of urgency to complete this development so that they could move on to the quantity production. Eventually, Bill did rise to the challenge and did describe in some detail how a series of parallel multi-processors receiving commands from a reduced instruction set controller would achieve the desired speed without sacrificing performance. This design was one of the choices Bill had discussed earlier with Fred Manning, the system engineer for the project.

Fred had considerable system engineering experience, and he very much enjoyed being in such great demand. His work on three projects in addition to Dynamo felt less like a burden and more like a plus. Although he knew that he was overcommitted and that his progress on Dynamo was behind schedule, he would not share that fact with Bill or with anyone else for that matter. He had learned over time that avoiding the inevitable confrontations that would ensue justified the lack of full honesty. Besides, Fred felt that he had an understanding with Bill about not being micromanaged; when push came to shove, he did seem to manage to deliver on his system engineering obligations. Fred felt that his situation was more the norm than the exception. When he looked around the System Engineering Division and when he looked around the parent organization, he saw much the same thing. He saw many dedicated, hard-working project team members rising to serve the needs of the mission by delivering on their commitments and not allowing themselves to become distracted by bureaucratic process.

June steered the conversation toward the subject of the customer. She told Bill of a conversation that she had overheard between the primary customers for the Dynamo signal processor. She told Bill about the apparent decision by these customers to adopt a new strategy whereby Dynamo would be used as a backup and not as their primary processor as was first planned. Bill could hardly believe what he was hearing; he had worked with these customers for years and thought he had an accurate understanding of what they needed. In fact, he was so sure of his relationship with these customers that he had virtually skipped the requirements definition and planning phases of his project, moving quickly into the concept development as a way to shorten substantially the schedule. This same type of time-saving approach had previously drawn praise from the customer and from the BOD; they appreciated his efficient use of scarce resources. He wondered how the customer could betray him like this. Additionally, he wondered about why now – just when things had gone badly with the BOD.

Lester Fields had felt quite satisfied with his career, having risen through the administration and finance ranks to increasingly important assignments. His current assignment as executive officer provided him the opportunity to sit on the BOD along with the functional department managers. His feeling about the Dynamo review was mixed. Having known Bill to be a capable project manager, he was reluctant to criticize his performance in an open forum. However, privately he was beginning to wonder if Bill's decisions over the past few years to forego project management training in favor of getting the job at hand done was serving him well. Perhaps it had; after all Bill had received a series of awards, which Lester had supported, for his heroic project management efforts.

Lester's recent assignments had been in organizations where projects routinely involved considerable risk. These were the types of projects where performance deviations and failures of fielded systems were difficult, if not impossible, to correct. He had become familiar with and an advocate for the use of a rigorous project management life cycle process as a way to deal with this degree of risk. Some of the other BOD members were showing interest in Lester's experience in this area. Lester was eager to demonstrate the value of this approach and had been working with Bill to apply this rigor to the Dynamo project. Bill had been following Lester's process since the beginning of the Dynamo project, and Lester was now considering briefing the BOD about this fact and using the Dynamo project as a demonstration of his approach. Bill's fractured review with the BOD was not helpful to Lester's strategy.

Sample Solutions

These sample solutions are provided to help readers advance to higher levels of learning and to assist readers in applying the information in this book. These sample solutions may be supplemented with additional solutions based on the readers' understanding of the information in this book and their own knowledge and experience.

Sample Solution Background

Character	Role
Dynamo	Project
Bill Bronson	Project Manager
BOD	Review Audience
June Simmons	Operations
Fred Manning	System Engineer
Customer	Priorities
Lester Fields	Executive Officer

Sample Solution 2.1

Underlying Problem Statement
Project manager having difficulty with BOD about project review
Project manager and BOD executives have different agendas
Project headed for trouble

Sample Solution 3.1

Additional Executive Actions		
What	**Why**	**How**
As determined by participant	As determined by participant	As determined by participant

Sample Solution 3.2

Action	Why
Top Actions	
Adhere to a suitable project management process	Alleviate opinion differences about scope of review
Behave like an executive – ask the right questions	Avoid inappropriate design questions when project has not progressed past requirements
Pick the right projects	Avoid apparent ambiguity about priority of Dynamo project
Develop/maintain close stakeholder/customer relationship	Address apparent ambiguity about priority of Dynamo project
Make sure projects are based on documented requirements	Avoid risk of skipping requirements definition phase
Ensure projects follow a documented plan	Avoid risk of skipping planning phase
Engage middle management help	No evidence of involvement
Establish and use job definition/performance standards	Avoid assigning insufficiently qualified project manager

Sample Solution 4.1

	Action	Barrier
Top Actions	Adhere to a suitable project management process	Maturity of organization may not support a commonly followed process
		Executive project management knowledge is varied and limited
		Level of readiness for change may be low
	Behave like an executive – ask the right questions	Viewpoints differ; executive likely unaware of the right questions
		Office politics may be coloring executive behavior; executive office may have an agenda

Sample Solution 4.2

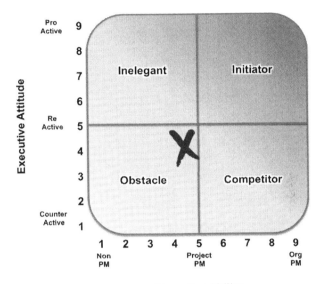

Sample Solution 5.1

Barrier	PM Step	Why
PM Steps To Help Executive		
Barrier	**PM Step**	**Why**
Maturity of organization may not support a commonly followed process	Behave like an alpha	Demonstrate project management excellence by openly adhering to a process and invite others to adopt
Executive project management knowledge is varied and limited	Use executive actions list with questions	Education of executives can alter their behavior
Level of readiness for change may be low	Communicate using business context	Frame needed project management changes in beneficial business terms and stress consequences of inaction
Viewpoints differ; executive likely unaware of the right questions	Use executive actions list with questions	Education of executives can alter their behavior
Office politics may be coloring executive behavior; executive office may have an agenda	Leverage sponsors and champions	Pre-formed sponsor relationships and positions can reduce competing agendas
All	Form a project management council	Very effective approach to amplify voice and aid implementation of actions

Index

69979482R00080

Made in the USA
San Bernardino, CA
24 February 2018